A book for Sportrivia buffs . . .

SPORTRIVIA

by
George Shane

VANTAGE PRESS
New York • Los Angeles

FIRST EDITION

Copyright © 1991 by George Shane

Published by Vantage Press, Inc.
516 West 34th Street, New York, New York 10001

Manufactured in the United States of America
ISBN: 0-533-08990-5

Library of Congress Catalog Card No.: 89-92920

Note

**With one or two exceptions all the individuals in-
cluded in** *Sportrivia* are no longer competitive in their
sports. In these cases the athletes have established records unsurpassed to this day.

How to Play Sportrivia

It's VERY simple.

Each right-hand page has 10 questions, and each left-hand page has a caricature of a famous athlete. At the end of each of the 1,000 Sportrivia questions you will find in brackets the word *answer* and a page number. Turn to this page and you will find a caricature of the sports great whose name is the correct answer to the question.

For example:

> 27. Baseball: He was married in 1954 to Hollywood's most glamorous actress. The marriage lasted 9 months. Who was the husband?
> (*answer p. 144*)

The answer to question 27 is on page 144. What could be simpler?

Sportrivia can be a useful reference book—or you can cut out the pages of your favorite stars and use them to paper your walls, locker, bus stop, et cetera.

1. **Soccer:** The NY Cosmos offered his W. German club over 2 million dollars for his services in 1977. Who was this expensive purchase? (*answer p.134*)

2. **Basketball:** _____ was the highest scoring guard in NBA history and its 3rd all time scorer, averaging 27 points per game. (*answer p.138*)

3. **Swimming:** When the Swimming Hall of Fame was established (1966) he was the first honoree. Who was this aquatic giant? (*answer p.86*)

4. **Baseball:** This future Yankee great made his pro debut in 1921 under the name of Lou Lewis. He was _____? (*answer p.184*)

5. **Football:** He was voted Canada's outstanding football player in 1966 and 1970. Who was this quarterback? (*answer p.88*)

6. **Figure Skating:** She was named Canada's Outstanding Athlete three times in four years: 1945, 1947 and 1948. Who was Canada's sweetheart? (*answer p.28*)

7. **Boxing:** Because of financial reverses, this ex-lightweight champion was forced to return to the ring (1932) after a 7 year layoff. (*answer p.194*)

8. **Tennis:** He led the US amateur team which in 1937, brought back the Davis Cup after the lapse of a decade. (*answer p.92*)

9. **Soccer:** Playing for Manchester United and the English international team, _____ was named, European Footballer of the Year in 1966. (*answer p.78*)

10. **Golf:** Only 5 ft. 7 in. and weighing about 130 lbs. he was nicknamed "Little Ben". What was his surname? (*answer p.84*)

CHRISTY MATHEWSON

Page 3

11. **Jockeys:** Immensely successful in North America he never won a race in Europe or down under (1930-61). (*answer p.152*)

12. **Swimming:** In 1967, he won an unprecedented 5 gold medals in the Pan American games. (*answer p.192*)

13. **Boxing:** Blinded in 1 eye, suffering from cataracts in the other, he was forced to retire in 1923. Who was this heavyweight? (*answer p.64*)

14. **Baseball:** In his rookie year (1936), he tied Dizzy Dean's single game strikeout record, fanning 17 Philadelphia Athletics. (*answer p.94*)

15. **Golf:** Famous as a golfer, this Englishman also played cricket, captained the Ganton soccer team in the early 1900's. (*answer p.26*)

16. **Football:** Very much a playboy and sex symbol, he was known as "Broadway Joe". What was his surname? (*answer p.150*)

17. **Boxing:** At 5 ft. 7 in. and weighing under 175 lbs., _____ was the shortest man ever to wear the world heavyweight crown. (*answer p.180*)

18. **Baseball:** He was voted the National League's Most Valuable Player in 1957 when his Braves defeated the NY Yankees in the World Series.(*answer p.82*)

19. **Football:** Born in the U.S. in 1940, this running back helped form the CFL Players' Association, became its president. (*answer p.130*)

20. **Basketball:** Coach Phog Allen of Kansas declared: " _____ is the greatest player of all time for his size". Whom was he speaking of? (*answer p.138*)

ALTHEA GIBSON

21. **Hockey:** Between 1967 and 1975, he won the NHL Most Valuable Player award 3 times. Who was this triple winner? (**answer p.100**)

22. **Tennis:** "The Battles of the Two Helens" riveted the attention of the sports world in the 30's. One was Helen Jacobs - who was the other? (**answer p.60**)

23. **Baseball:** In 1939 this black slugger hit more home runs in Washington's Griffith Stadium than all the AL right-handed hitters combined. He was _____? (**answer p.198**)

24. **Football:** In 1975, this fullback set up (in Saskatchewan) his Foundation for the Handicapped. (**answer p.130**)

25. **Boxing:** He enlisted in 1915, later won the light heavyweight championship of the US Expeditionary Forces. Who was the Marine who landed so many winning punches? (**answer p.24**)

26. **Basketball:** In 1966, he became the first black coach of a major league franchise. His name was _____? (**answer p.8**)

27. **Baseball:** He was married in 1954 to Hollywood's most glamorous actress. The marriage lasted 9 months. Who was the husband? (**answer p.144**)

28. **Figure Skating:** This US skater became known as the "Ice Queen" in the sixties. Who was she? (**answer p.128**)

29. **Golf:** His real name was Eugene Saraceni. To what did he change it? (**answer p.6**)

30. **Hockey:** He ran up a total of 1,219 points in 18 years, 1953-71, in the NHL .... 4th highest on record. (**answer p.174**)

GENE SARAZEN

31. **Golf:** At the age of 28, he announced his retirement from competitive golf, rocking the sports world. He was _____? (**answer p.176**)

32. **Jockeys:** Setting the longest endurance record amongst jockeys, he won over a million dollars in 8 different years. (**answer p.18**)

33. **Hockey:** In one season, 1965-66 this Chicago player captured the Hart Trophy, the Art Ross Trophy and the Lady Byng Trophy. (**answer p.178**)

34. **Boxing:** He held the heavyweight championship longer than any other fighter .... 11 years, 8 months and 7 days (1937-1949). (**answer p.110**)

35. **Soccer:** At the age of 20, he got his first "cap", playing against Scotland in 1958. The cap fitted - who wore it? (**answer p.78**)

36. **Baseball:** He moved into pro ball in 1950 with the Indianapolis Clowns - a team which never played in Indianapolis. (**answer p.82**)

37. **Football:** After retirement as a pro, he hosted "Saturday Night Live" on TV. Who was this TV luminary? (**answer p.120**)

38. **Baseball:** Until it was eclipsed by Pete Rose, he held the big league record for stolen bases. Who was this base thief? (**answer p.12**)

39. **Boxing:** In 1964, a convert to Mohammedanism, this heavyweight changed his name - and won the world title. What is the name by which the world knows him? (**answer p.162**)

40. **Baseball:** As a Washington Senator, _____ won 20 games or more over 10 seasons (1910-20). (**answer p.102**)

BILL RUSSELL

41. **Soccer:** In his first year in the North American Soccer League (1979) _____ was voted the league's Most Valuable Player? (*answer p.10*)

42. **Boxing:** Born in 1858 in Boston, he became famous as "The Boston Strong Boy". What was this heavyweight's name? (*answer p.172*)

43. **Hockey:** After a horrendous injury in March 1950, he was told he would never play pro hockey again - in 1951 he won the NHL scoring championship. (*answer p.136*)

44. **Football:** Born in Texas (1914), he led Texas Christian U. to a national championship and The Rose Bowl in 1936. (*answer p.182*)

45. **Tennis:** Starting in 1933 he won 3 straight Wimbledon singles titles. Who was this English star? (*answer p.72*)

46. **Hockey:** A famous Boston defenseman said: "He's the hardest player in the NHL to stop." Of which Canadien forward was Eddie Shore speaking? (*answer p.114*)

47. **Baseball:** _____ pitched the only opening-day big league no-hitter .... against the Chicago White Sox in 1940. (*answer p.94*)

48. **Hockey:** He retired from pro sport in 1937, was elected Liberal M. P. P. for the Toronto area where he was born (1900). (*answer p.158*)

49. **Football:** After this quarterback's retirement, he was offered $100,000 by the B.C. Lions, $200,000 by the Memphis Southmen to return. Who said no to both. (*answer p.166*)

50. **Soccer:** The Portuguese nicknamed this UK star "El Beatle". Who was this non-musical beatle? (*answer p.200*)

JOHAN
CRUYFF

51. **Football:** _____ was the best passer in CFL history, throwing for 50, 535 yards, 20,000 more than his nearest rival. (*answer p.88*)

52. **Baseball:** Signed in 1935 by the Cleveland Indians at the age of 17, his bonus was a dollar bill and a baseball. (*answer p.94*)

53. **Tennis:** In 1968, she won her 3rd Wimbledon singles title, then teamed up to win the women's and mixed doubles. (*answer p.196*)

54. **Boxing:** In 2 pre-title bouts in 1918 he knocked out Fred Fulton in 18 seconds and Carl Morris in 14 seconds. Who was this heavyweight? (*answer p.108*)

55. **Soccer:** Born in 1947, _____ led his teams (Amsterdam and Barcelona) to 6 league championships, 3 European Cups and a World Cup final. (*answer p.10*)

56. **Hockey:** His nickname was rather surprisingly, "Jake the Snake". Who was this goalkeeper? (*answer p.186*)

57. **Baseball:** An outstanding graduate of Bucknell U., this NY Giant pitcher became the 1st US baseball idol, was featured in many advertisements. (*answer p.2*)

58. **Soccer:** His real name is Edson Arantes do Nascimento but the world calls him _____? (*answer p.66*)

59. **Football:** As a teenager he was known as "The Wheaton Iceman", lugging great blocks of ice up and down stairs. Who was this iceman? (*answer p.140*)

60. **Football:** When he graduated from high school (1955), over 40 colleges offered him an athletic scholarship. _____ chose Syracuse U. and no scholarship. (*answer p.96*)

TY COBB

61. **Baseball:** He was the only hitter to ever hit a fair ball out of Yankee Stadium (580 ft). What was this slugger's name. (*answer p.198*)

62. **Track:** He was the only athlete to ever win both the Olympic pentathlon and decathlon (1912). Name him. (*answer p.30*)

63. **Basketball:** During his 1961-62 season with the Harlem Globetrotters, he averaged a record 50.4 points per game. (*answer p.188*)

64. **Hockey:** _____ is one of the few hockey players (Montreal Canadiens) to have received the Order of Canada. (*answer p.174*)

65. **Boxing:** In a 10-round decision, he won the world heavyweight championship in 1926. Who was this New Yorker? (*answer p.24*)

66. **Golf:** In 1914 he won the U S Open for the first time. (*answer p.20*)

67. **Baseball:** After his retirement, pitcher _____ took a job in 1941 as a baseball broadcaster from Sportsman's Park, St. Louis. (*answer p.132*)

68. **Tennis:** This ex-Wimbledon and US national champion was appointed New Jersey State Athletic Commissioner, ran for the state senate in the 60's. (*answer p.4*)

69. **Basketball:** "We got stuck with the greatest player in the league when we drew his name out of a hat". Of whom was Red Auerbach speaking? *answer p.164*)

70. **Golf:** _____ won his first U.S. Open in 1948 (at the age of 36) - the purse was $1,500.00. (*answer p.84*)

ROCKET RICHARD

71. **Baseball:** Chosen by Brooklyn's Branch Rickey to break major league baseball's color bar _____ was brought to the Dodgers in 1947. (***answer p.56***)

72. **Football:** _____ quarterbacked the Edmonton Eskimos to 3 consecutive Grey Cups 1954-56. (***answer p.70***)

73. **Swimming:** Born (1904) in Windber, Pa., he won his first international championship at age 18, went on to capture 55 more. (***answer p.86***)

74. **Track:** In 1929, he won 21 of 22 indoor sprints during a 21-day US tour. Who was this Canadian speedster? (***answer p.50***)

75. **Hockey:** His dazzling skating earned him the nickname "The Rocket". Who was this supersonic speedster? (***answer p.14***)

76. **Swimming:** Though he signed (1972) a reported $6 million movie contract, he was a flop as an actor. Who was this failed cinema star? (***answer p.192***)

77. **Soccer:** Born in 1946 in Munich, this West German star noted for his fair, clean play was not once sent off the field. (***answer p.134***)

78. **Figure Skating:** Having won 5 consecutive US national championships, she turned professional in 1969. (***answer p.128***)

79. **Baseball:** "I wouldn't trade _____ even up for anybody in baseball". To which NY Giants' player was manager Leo Durocher referring? ***answer p.170***)

80. **Tennis:** She first won the US singles title at 17 (1923), defeating veteran champion Molla Mallory. (***answer p.60***)

JACK KRAMER

81. **Football:** _____ led the Washington Redskins to 5 division titles in 10 years as well as 2 NFL crowns. (*answer p.182)*

82. **Boxing:** For his first pro fight (1911) this lightweight received $10 and a black eye ... the only one in his ring career. (*answer p.194)*

83. **Tennis:** Her first and only coach was her French father who developed her accuracy by making her use a coin as a target. (*answer p.142)*

84. **Boxing:** Born in 1878, he became known as "Little Arthur, the Galveston Giant". Who was he? (*answer p.90)*

85. **Tennis:** In 1953, _____ set up World Tennis, Inc. - with himself as president and his mother as secretary-treasurer. (*answer p.16)*

86. **Hockey:** With his 2 sons, he moved to the Hartford Whalers in 1977 - they were the only former WHA team to make the NHL play-offs. (*answer p.136)*

87. **Hockey:** Goalkeepers rarely win the Hart Trophy (NHL's Most Valuable Player) - he did it in 1962. His name was _____? (*answer p.186)*

88. **Football:** During his 13 years in the CFL (1963-1976), this fullback held as many as 44 records. He was _____? (*answer p.130)*

89. **Hockey:** He won the Vezina Trophy (best goalie) 3 times with Detroit and once (shared) with Toronto. (*answer p.76)*

90. **Track:** This Brantford, Ontario marathoner outran a horse in a 12-mile race in 1906. Who was he? (*answer p.126)*

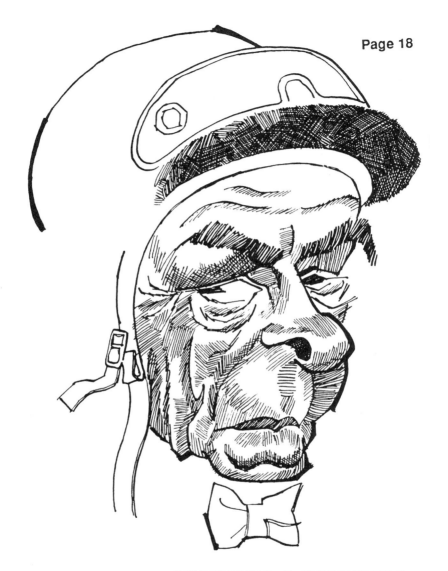

JOHNNY LONGDEN

91. **Figure Skating:** She married Tom King in 1955, quit pro skating and took up riding, breeding, and showing horses. (*answer p.28*)

92. **Baseball:** After finishing his pitching career in 1927, he went on to Newark in the International League as manager. (*answer p.102*)

93. **Hockey:** Within 4 years of his joining Boston, he led his team from last place to the Stanley Cup in 1970. Who was this defenseman? (*answer p.100*)

94. **Baseball:** Though born in Nebraska, this pitcher's middle name was that of a large Ohio city. What was his full name? (*answer p.156*)

95. **Football:** His nickname was "Orange Juice" shortened to "The Juice". What was his real name? (*answer p.120*)

96. **Hockey:** Born (1902) in Mitchell, Ontario, he became known as "The Stratford Streak". Who was this skating streaker? (*answer p.114*)

97. **Golf:** Because of his elegant dress and short stature he became known as "The Little Squire". He was _____? (*answer p.6*)

98. **Football:** In 1969, _____ won the CFL outstanding player award, the Schenley Trophy, the Lou Marsh Trophy, the Canadian Press Athlete of the Year award - then retired. (*answer p.166*)

99. **Track:** Famous for running with a stopwatch, this Finn would throw it into the infield at the start of the last lap. (*answer p.190*)

100. **Tennis:** He sparked the US team to a 7-year reign in Davis Cup play (1920-27), won 13 of his 14 singles matches. (*answer p.46*)

WALTER HAGEN

101. **Baseball:** He was signed (1951) by Bill Veeck of the St. Louis Browns, who provided him with a rocking chair in the bullpen. What was this rock star's name? (*answer p.68*)

102. **Tennis:** He was the only player to ever win the Grand Slam of tennis twice. Who was he? (*answer p.146*)

103. **Skating:** Having won every possible title in figure skating, _____ starred in 7 Hollywood films, earning more than $1,000,000.00. (*answer p.74*)

104. **Boxing:** The only boxer to ever hold 3 world championships simultaneously: featherweight, lightweight and welterweight, he was _____? (*answer p.148*)

105. **Golf:** Born (1912) in Dublin, Texas, he didn't win his first tournament till he was 26. (*answer p.84*)

106. **Football:** In his career as a Chicago Bear, _____ threw 1,744 passes for 14, 686 yards and 137 touchdowns. (*answer p.112*)

107. **Boxing:** His motto was "float like a butterfly, sting like a bee". Who was this poetic US boxer? (*answer p.162*)

108. **Swimming:** In his 2nd Olympics (1968), _____ won a relay gold and an individual 200 meter freestyle silver medal-then retired. (*answer p.54*)

109. **Hockey:** Not only did he set a goal-scoring record (54), he also hit an all-time NHL point record of 97 in 1966. (*answer p.178*)

110. **Football:** He was Saskatchewan's head coach for 2 years (1979-80). The record: won 4, lost 28. (*answer p.88*)

PETE ROSE

111. **Baseball:** Next to Satchell Paige, _____ was the highest paid black player in baseball - averaging $7,000-10,000 a year when white players were earning 10 or 15 times as much. (**answer p.198**)

112. **Basketball:** In 1971, converted to Mohammedanism, he changed his name from Ferdinand Lewis Alcindor to _____? (**answer p.40**)

113. **Football:** When this quarterback retired in 1968, he was the CFL's leading all-time scorer with 750 points. (**answer p.70**)

114. **Soccer:** He made his international debut at 17 against Austria in 1945. His team won 5-2. Who was this Hungarian player? (**answer p.106**)

115. **Boxing:** In San Diego, Cal., this heavyweight fought 2 challengers in one evening (1907). He knocked them both out. (**answer p.180**)

116. **Tennis:** She won the US Women's title 7 times in 8 years (1923-31), losing only in 1926 due to an appendicitis attack. (**answer p.60**)

117. **Jockeys:** Unusually tall, for a jockey, (5 ft. 7 in.) he is known as the "Long Fella". What was his name? (**answer p.98**)

118. **Golf:** He was the inventor of the later-outlawed "croquet putt". What was this innovator's name? (**answer p.124**)

119. **Baseball:** Born 1887 in Humboldt, Kansas, this fireball pitcher set an all-time major league record of 113 shutouts. (**answer p.102**)

120. **Boxing:** Fritzie Zivic took away his welterweight crown in 1940, beat him again the following year. (**answer p.148**)

GENE TUNNEY

121. Tennis: Taking up tennis only at 19, he won the Middlesex junior doubles crown (1928) - within 5 years he was the Wimbledon champion. (*answer p.72)*

122. Soccer: He retired from British soccer in 1972 declaring: "I am a physical and mental wreck. I've been drinking too much". Who said it? (*answer p.200)*

123. Baseball: A former pitcher, this Yankee outfielder hit a career total of 714 home runs. What was this ex-pitcher's name? (*answer p.44)*

124. Soccer: "Pele brought American soccer to 60% of its potential. My job is to raise it to 75%." What European player said it? (*answer p.10)*

125. Golf: _____ was the host in the 60's for TV's Wonderful World of Golf. (*answer p.6)*

126. Baseball: When he was 19 (1930), a St. Louis Cardinal scout signed him for a $300 bonus and $1800 a year. (*answer p.132)*

127. Hockey: Pro hockey's first superstar (1906-1922) rejected an offer to endorse a brand of underwear ... on his wife's insistence. Who was this modest marvel? (*answer p.52)*

128. Jockeys: _____ has won over $6 million in his career and has the highest winning percentage among name jockeys (24%). (*answer p.58)*

129. Tennis: She turned pro in 1973, later won $205,000 in the Virginia Slims Tournament. (*answer p.118)*

130. Baseball: He played 2nd base with Brooklyn in 6 world series against the Yankees - they won once in 1955. (*answer p.56)*

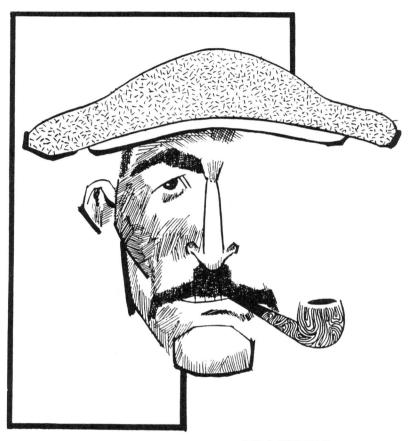

HARRY
VARDON

131. Soccer: In 1965 he was knighted "for services to football" - the first active player to win this honor.... Sir _____. (*answer p.42*)

132. Baseball: A huge statue of _____ was erected near Forbes Field in Pittsburgh to honor this great Pirate player (1955). (*answer p.122*)

133. Boxing: This heavyweight champion appeared (1890) in a hugely successful melodrama entitled Honest Hearts and Willing Hands. Name this part-time actor. (*answer p.172*)

134. Soccer: He was the Spanish League's top scorer 5 times, played 31 times internationally for Spain. (*answer p.116*)

135. Baseball: His major league career was spent on a single team which won 4 consecutive AL pennants from 1936 to 1939. (*answer p.144*)

136. Tennis: This tall redhead, aged 23, earned the then staggering sum of $148,000 during his first year as a pro. (*answer p.92*)

137. Hockey: Despite a growing illness (1924-25), this goalkeeper established a record of 1.9 goals per game - the best in the NHL. (*answer p.34*)

138. Baseball: This outfielder led the Negro American League in 1951 with a batting average of .467. His name was _____? (*answer p.82*)

139. Tennis: He and Bunny Austin broke France's hold on the Davis Cup in 1933, held it for 3 successful defenses. (*answer p.72*)

140. Hockey: In the 1967-68 season, he set an NHL record for defensemen, scoring 85 points. (*answer p.100*)

BARBARA ANN
SCOTT

141. **Figure Skating:** Born in California in 1949, she only began skating at the age of 9 - won her first competition 2 years later. (**answer p.128**)

142. **Track:** In 1934 he set new world records for the indoor mile (4:08.4) and the outdoor mile (4:06.4). Who was the double-sided record holder? (**answer p.154**)

143. **Hockey:** Playing for Detroit, Houston and Hartford, _____ was the first player to reach the 1000 point mark. (**answer p.136**)

144. **Tennis:** After a protracted illness she returned to competitive tennis. An inspiring letter from actress Carole Lombard sparked her decision. (**answer p.38**)

145. **Football:** In 9 years (1957-65), this Cleveland fullback led the NFL 8 times in rushing. Who was this rushing star? (**answer p.96**)

146. **Jockeys:** His nickname was "Old Banana Nose". _____ was never just one of the bunch. (**answer p.152**)

147. **Tennis:** In 1960 (aged 17), she and Karen Hantze won the Wimbledon doubles crown - the youngest team to do it. (**answer p.196**)

148. **Hockey:** During an 18-game season (1917-18) with Vancouver, _____ scored a record 32 goals, 6 in a single game. (**answer p.52**)

149. **Boxing:** Born in 1914 in Lafayette, Ala., this future Detroit heavyweight won a National AAV championship (1934) as a light heavyweight. (**answer p.110**)

150. **Football:** After retiring as a player (1935), he served for 3 years as an assistant to George Halas, coach of the Chicago Bears. (**answer p.140**)

JIM THORPE

151. Baseball: On retirement (1960), he was the major's highest-paid player at $125,000 a year, with a lifetime .344 batting average. (***answer p.32)***

152. Football: An All-American from Mississippi State, _____ scored the decisive touchdown in the Edmonton Eskimos 1954 Grey Cup win. (***answer p.70)***

153. Boxing: He was nicknamed "Ruby Robert" because his freckles turned crimson during matches. What was this English-born fighter's name? (***answer p.80)***

154. Jockeys: His first official win was in Salt Lake City (1927) on a gelding named Hugo K Asher. Who was the horse's rider? (***answer p.18)***

155. Baseball: He was named the NL's Most Valuable Player in 1954, again in 1965. Who was this NY Giant? (***answer p.170)***

156. Soccer: As manager-coach of Boca (Argentina) juniors (1969), he led them to the National Championship against River Plate. (***answer p.116)***

157. Golf: He holds the record for the last 36 holes of the PGA tournament ... only 122 strokes. (***answer p.124)***

158. Boxing: _____ was the only fighter to ever hold 6 world championships. (***answer p.36)***

159. Tennis: He was called Big Bill to distinguish him from his fiercest rival, Little Bill. What was his surname? (***answer p.46)***

160. Track: _____ scored 8,412.96 points out of a possible 10,000 in the 1912 Olympic decathlon - a record that held for 50 years. (***answer p.30)***

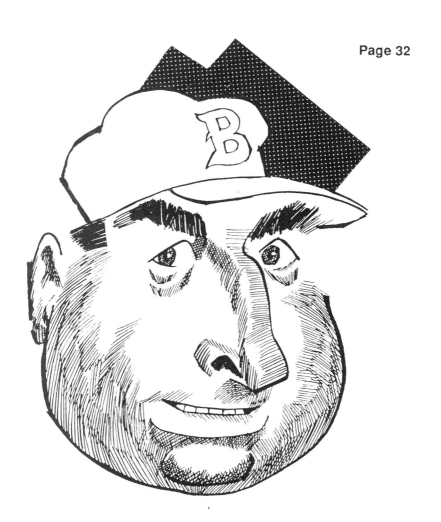

TED WILLIAMS

161. **Golf:** He captured the US Golfers' Ass'n. title in 1900 - was 2nd in 1913 - to American Francis Ouimet. Name this English champion. (***answer p.26***)

162. **Figure Skating:** Married to college sweetheart Dr. Greg Jenkins, she achieved success in sportswear design for McCall's in the 70's. (***answer p.128***)

163. **Boxing:** He regained the welterweight title from Barney Ross in 1934. Who was this Canadian champion? (***answer p.48***)

164. **Soccer:** Matt Busby gave him his first professional chance against Charlton Athletic in 1956 - oddly appropriate. What was his name? (***answer p.78***)

165. **Baseball:** This pitcher's 373 victories tied him with another, earlier National Leaguer for the greatest number of NL wins. Who was he? (***answer p.156***)

166. **Track:** Badly burned in a rural schoolhouse fire at the age of 8, _____ was told by his doctor that he would never walk again. (***answer p.154***)

167. **Basketball:** He was known as "The Houdini of the Hardwood". What was this magician's name? (***answer p.164***)

168. **Golf:** He was involved in a head-on car crash in 1949. Doctors saved his life but told _____ he'd never play again. (***answer p.84***)

169. **Figure Skating:** She was the first skater in the 20's 30's and 40's to dance on skates, using ballet techniques and costumes. (***answer p.74***)

170. **Hockey:** There were 10 children in this hockey family and one of his brothers was a member of Toronto's famous Kid Line. Whose family was it? (***answer p.158***)

GEORGES
VEZINA

171. **Football:** An NFL fullback who never missed a game, he went on to play film roles, notably in "The Dirty Dozen" with Lee Marvin. (***answer p.96***)

172. **Tennis:** At Wimbledon in 1926, she kept Britain's Queen Mary waiting for an hour, thereby provoking a storm of criticism. (***answer p.142***)

173. **Baseball:** Considered baseball's best-ever shortstop, _____ batted over .300 for 15 straight years, led the NL in stolen bases 5 times. (***answer p.122***)

174. **Hockey:** A bridge enthusiast, a gourmet cook, a landscape painter, this mostly Montreal goalkeeper was also widely known as a master knitter. (***answer p.186***)

175. **Hockey:** He was the Calder Cup winner with Detroit Red Wings in 1951. Who was this Rookie of the Year? (***answer p.76***)

176. **Golf:** Although he won every major title and tournament, amateur and professional, _____ never earned a penny playing golf. (***answer p.176***)

177. **Soccer:** At the tender age of 15 he joined Amsterdam Ajax (1962). What was this youngster's name? (***answer p.10***)

178. **Boxing:** _____ won the world heavyweight championship in 1919, knocking out Jess Willard in the 3rd round. (***answer p.108***)

179. **Jockeys:** He holds the record for stake race wins - over 660, better than 100 more than his nearest rival. (***answer p.58***)

180. **Soccer:** _____ led England to the World Cup in 1968, was named European Footballer of the Year. (***answer p.200***)

SUGAR RAY ROBINSON

181. **Football:** Ottawa traded him when they chose to use Russ Jackson as their quarterback in 1962. He was _____? (*answer p.88*)

182. **Soccer:** _____ last professional score was with his original team, Stoke City (1961) - it was the winning goal, moving the team up to the first division. (*answer p.42*)

183. **Jockeys:** He won a record of 549 stake races on US tracks, starting in 1930. Who was this stake-lover? (*answer p.152*)

184. **Boxing:** In an effort to win his 4th ring crown, he fought to a draw with middleweight champion Ceferino Garcia (1940). (*answer p.148*)

185. **Swimming:** In the late 20's and early 30's he won 18 AAV championships, set 16 World and 35 national records. (*answer p.160*)

186. **Football:** He became very closely identified with TV commercials promoting a brand of pantyhose - who was he? (*answer p.150*)

187. **Golf:** In 1913, 20 year-old American Francis Ouimet won the US Open. This golfer finished 4th. Who was he? (*answer p.20*)

188. **Baseball:** The NY Yankees obtained him from the San Francisco Seals for $25,000 and 5 players (1934). (*answer p.144*)

189. **Boxing:** This ring marvel won the world middleweight title 5 times in all. He was _____? (*answer p.36*)

190. **Soccer:** Unfounded rumors reported _____ killed in fighting during the Hungarian uprising of 1956. (*answer p.106*)

ALICE MARBLE

191. **Boxing:** At 37 (1917), he lost to younger, bigger, Fred Fulton. His left eye was permanently blinded but he fought for several more years. (*answer p.64*)

192. **Track:** This famous US miler duelled with New Zealand's Jack Lovelock and Britain's Sydney Wooderson in the 1930's, each lowering the mile record in turn. Who was he? (*answer p.154*)

193. **Boxing:** Born (1942) in Louisville, Ky. _____ won the Olympic light-heavyweight title in 1960. (*answer p.162*)

194. **Jockeys:** He won a record 29 classics (1947-85) including the Two Thousand Guineas 4 times and the One Thousand Guineas twice. (*answer p.98*)

195. **Soccer:** In 1958, he scored 2 goals against Sweden helping his Brazilian team to win the first of 4 World Cups. (*answer p.66*)

196. **Football:** This Southern California halfback, later a Buffalo Bill, was able to run the 100 yards in 9.4 seconds. (*answer p.120*)

197. **Hockey:** "The Big Train" was his popular nickname. Off-ice what was his real name? (*answer p.158*)

198. **Basketball:** He was selected to the All-NBA first team 3 times, the second All-NBA team 7 times. (*answer p.8*)

199. **Boxing:** He fought Joe Frazier 3 times, won 2, lost 1. Who was this heavyweight champion? (*answer p.162*)

200. **Tennis:** In the early 1950's he played 123 pro matches in 1 year against Pancho Gonzales - and won 96. He was _____ ? (*answer p.16*)

KAREEM ABDUL-JABBAR

201. **Golf:** Though not the first to use it, he was the golfer who popularized the over-lapping grip which bears his name, _____. (*answer p.26*)

202. **Football:** "Slinging Sammy" was his nickname but he got it playing baseball not football. What was his full name? (*answer p.182*)

203. **Basketball:** Cincinnati coach Bob Cousy and he didn't get on well so he accepted a trade to the Milwaukee Bucks in 1970. Who was this tradee? (*answer p.138*)

204. **Boxing:** Born in Belfast in 1907, he defeated 13 men who had at some time been world champions. Who was this Canadian welterweight? (*answer p.48*)

205. **Tennis:** To decide who was the world's best player, _____ agreed to a match against Helen Wills Moody (1926), defeated her in straight sets. (*answer p.142*)

206. **Basketball:** Against his wishes, he was named to the Basketball Hall of Fame in 1974. Who was this refusenik? (*answer p.8*)

207. **Golf:** He retired from tournament play in 1937, having won more major pro titles than any golfer until Jack Nicklaus. (*answer p.20*)

208. **Jockeys:** Winner of 5 Kentucky Derbies, he was the US national jockey champion 4 times in 6 years. (*answer p.168*)

209. **Baseball:** Despite going hitless in his first 22 trips to the plate, this outfielder won the major league Rookie of the Year award in 1952. (*answer p.170*)

210. **Soccer:** During his 11 years with Real Madrid they won 5 European Cup medals, 1 World Cup championship and 8 Spanish League medals. (*answer p.116*)

STANLEY MATTHEWS

211. **Tennis:** Sugar Ray Robinson and his wife took this teenager into their home, launched her on a tennis career. Who was this New Yorker? (***answer p.4)***

212. **Boxing:** After retirement from the ring (1940), _____ became an ordained Baptist minister in St. Louis, Mo. in 1951. (***answer p.148)***

213. **Baseball:** In 1973, he tied Wee Willie Keeler's NL record of hitting in 44 straight games. (***answer p.22)***

214. **Football:** This American-born import told his Regina, Saskatchewan fans: "I came, I played, I stayed". Who was this Caesar? (***answer p.130)***

215. **Hockey:** He was given a tryout at the age of 15 (1943) by the NY Rangers but did not make a deep impression. (***answer p.136)***

216. **Golf:** He won the British Amateur and British Open each 3 times, the US Amateur 5 times, the US Open 4 times (1923-30). (***answer p.176)***

217. **Baseball:** A movie, "The Pride of St. Louis", was made about him. It starred actor Dan Dailey. Whose life was it based on? (***answer p.132)***

218. **Boxing:** His last heavyweight title defense - and pro fight - was a KO of Tommy Heeney of New Zealand in 1928. (***answer p.24)***

219. **Basketball:** On April 5, 1984, this centre reached a total of 31,421 lifetime points, the highest-ever in NBA history. (***answer p.40)***

220. **Hockey:** After only a year as a coach in Quebec (1973-74), _____ left to play goal for the Edmonton Oilers. (***answer p.186)***

BABE RUTH

221. **Boxing:** This Canadian heavyweight was his own manager and earned $208,954 during his ring career which began in 1899. (*answer p.180*)

222. **Soccer:** In 1972, _____ was forced to withdraw from an international match in Belfast due to death threats against him. (*answer p.200*)

223. **Football:** After 3 seasons with the Toronto Argonauts, he moved to the B.C. Lions, became general manager and was fired (1970) after 2 years. Who was the firee? (*answer p.70*)

224. **Hockey:** Always cool and even-tempered, this Montreal goaltender was known as "The Chicoutimi Cucumber". What was his non-vegetarian name? (*answer p.34*)

225. **Baseball:** Faster than Walter Johnson? This Cleveland hurler's fastball was timed at 98.6 m.p.h. Who was he? (*answer p.94*)

226. **Soccer:** _____ was the first to win the English Footballer of the Year award, introduced in 1948, won it again 15 years later. (*answer p.42*)

227. **Football:** Winner of the Governor-General's Academic Medal for Excellence, Ottawa's _____ led his team to 3 Grey Cups over 11 years (1958-69). (*answer p.166*)

228. **Baseball:** He pitched for the St. Louis Browns in 1952 (aged 46), was the league's top relief pitcher with a 12-10 record and 10 saves. (*answer p.68*)

229. **Tennis:** In 1971, _____ became the first female athlete to earn over $100,000 a year. (*answer p.196*)

230. **Boxing:** After serving in the US Merchant Marine in World War II, he became a referee - collapsed and died in the ring (1947). (*answer p.194*)

BILL
TILDEN

231. Hockey: Playing as a defenseman, he scored 5 goals in 1 game for Ottawa in the Stanley Cup final of 1907. (***answer p.52***)

232. Boxing: Coached by "Pop Foster", he ended ex-lightweight champion Benny Leonard's comeback career by a knockout in 1932. (***answer p.48***)

233. Baseball: "He was not only the greatest catcher, but the greatest ball player I ever saw." said Ray Campanella... of whom? (***answer p.198***)

234. Tennis: After 2 consecutive victories at Forest Hills (1946-47) and capturing the singles title at Wimbledon, he turned pro in 1947. (***answer p.16***)

235. Track: At the age of 34 (1931), he astounded the world by running 2 miles in 8:59.5 and 6 miles in 29:36.6 - both new records. (***answer p.190***)

236. Football: His nickname was "The Little Assassin of Taylor Field". What was this killer's name? (***answer p.88***)

237. Baseball: This Yankee 1st baseman accepted 20,598 fielding chances, made only 194 errors (1925-1939) (***answer p.184***)

238. Hockey: This Montreal Canadien won the NHL Hart Trophy in 1956 and 1964, played on 10 Stanley Cup winners. (***answer p.174***)

239. Jockeys: He was born in Wakefield, England in 1907, took after his miner father who was only 4 ft. 9 in. tall. (***answer p.18***)

240. Tennis: She was the first black woman to win both the French and Italian Opens in 1956. (***answer p.4***)

JIMMY McLARNIN

241. **Football:** Saskatchewan's _____ missed only half a dozen games in his 13 years as a CFL fullback, played half a season with a fractured leg. (*answer p.130*)

242. **Tennis:** Often called the greatest player in history, this Californian preferred baseball as a boy, later adapted his baseball swing to tennis. (*answer p.92*)

243. **Hockey:** In 1970, he was named Canada's Athlete of the Year, Sportsman of the Year by Sports Illustrated. His name was _____? (*answer p.100*)

244. **Boxing:** He came out of retirement in 1950 to challenge for the heavyweight championship. _____ lost a 15-round decision to Ezzard Charles. (*answer p.110*)

245. **Football:** Born 1943 in Beaver Falls, Pa., he led the local high school team to its first interscholastic title in 35 years. (*answer p.150*)

246. **Basketball:** This 7 ft. 1 in. center's nickname was "The Big Dipper". Who was he? (*answer p.188*)

247. **Soccer:** This European star played alongside Pele on the NY Cosmos for a short time in 1977. (*answer p.134*)

248. **Boxing:** Starting in his 3rd pro year (1914), this lightweight fought 154 bouts over the next 9 years - without a single loss. (*answer p.194*)

249. **Track:** This marathon champion was born 1887 on the Six Nations Reserve near Brantford, Ontario. (*answer p.126*)

250. **Tennis:** She was nicknamed "The Arm" by Rosie Casals. What was her court name? (*answer p.118*)

PERCY WILLIAMS

251. **Baseball:** In a poll of sportswriters in 1969, _____ was named "The Greatest Living Player". though no longer active. (*answer p.144*)

252. **Track:** A poll of leading track-and-field coaches, experts and historians named this Ohio sprinter as the greatest runner of all time. He was _____? (*answer p.104*)

253. **Baseball:** This outfielder made himself so popular in Minneapolis that the NY Giants ran full-page ads of apology to local fans when they drafted _____ in 1952. (*answer p.170*)

254. **Basketball:** Arnold "Red" Auerbach traded Ed McCauley and Cliff Hagen to St. Louis for _____ (1956). (*answer p.8*)

255. **Soccer:** In his 17 years with Manchester United (1956-73), he sparked them to 3 League championships, 3 FA Cup finals. (*answer p.78*)

256. **Baseball:** "There is a catcher any big league team would like to buy for $200,000 ... he can do everything. He hits the ball a mile." Of whom was Walter Johnson speaking? (*answer p.198*)

257. **Golf:** The first American to capture the British Open (1922) _____ won it a record of 4 times. (*answer p.20*)

258. **Baseball:** His lifetime record of 373 wins set a NL record (later tied by another pitching great). He was _____? (*answer p.2*)

259. **Soccer:** This Stoke City forward retired (1965) aged 50, but continued to play - and coach - as an amateur into his 70's. (*answer p.42*)

260. **Tennis:** _____'s first pro match was against fellow-American Ellesworth Vines in 1939. (*answer p.92*)

CYCLONE TAYLOR

261. **Soccer:** The NY Cosmos offered him $1 million to come out of European retirement but the LA Aztecs topped them at $1.4 million. (*answer p.10*)

262. **Boxing:** He lost his welterweight title for the 2nd time to Barney Ross (1935) in a decision Gene Tunney called "a disgrace", scoring it 13-2 for him. (*answer p.48*)

263. **Tennis:** In 1926 she signed the first pro tour contract with C. C. Pyle (Red Grange's promoter) for a fabulous $50,000. (*answer p.142*)

264. **Hockey:** He led Montreal to the 1916 Stanley Cup against the Portland Rosebuds, received a bonus of $238 for the feat. (*answer p.34*)

265. **Track:** _____ was told (1912) by Swedish King Gustav V: "You, sir, are the greatest athlete in the world". (*answer p.30*)

266. **Hockey:** "L'homme-éclair," who was _____, scored an unheard-of 40 goals in 44 games in the NHL's 1929-30 season. (*answer p.114*)

267. **Swimming:** Including 3 in relay races, he won a total of 7 gold medals in the 1972 Munich Olympics. (*answer p.192*)

268. **Baseball:** His nickname was "The Georgia Peach", albeit a sour one. What was his name? (*answer p.12*)

269. **Hockey:** This right-winger was the 1st NHL player to score 50 goals in 50 games. Who was this Canadian star? (*answer p.14*)

270. **Golf:** Born (1902) in Harrison, N.Y., _____ won more PGA championship matches (67) than any other golfer. (*answer p.6*)

DON
SCHOLLANDER

271. **Tennis:** She turned down a $100,000 offer to become a pro (1938) because she regarded tennis "as a diversion, not a career". Who was this determined amateur? (*answer p.60*)

272. **Soccer:** He played for Manchester over 10 seasons, notched 135 goals in 349 games, led the league twice in scoring. (*answer p.200*)

273. **Hockey:** He won the NHL goal-scoring trophy 7 times, was the point leader 3 times and was named to the All-Star team 12 times in 15 years. (1957-72). (*answer p.178*)

274. **Baseball:** In 1962 the NY Mets offered San Francisco $650,000 for this player. They didn't get him till 10 years later. (*answer p.170*)

275. **Boxing:** The shortest heavyweight title defense on record was this champion's KO of Jem Roche in 1 minute and 28 seconds. (*answer p.180*)

276. **Jockeys:** He was the 5th North American rider to reach the figure of over 4000 winners (1970). (*answer p.168*)

277. **Track:** This ex-Olympian gold medalist set a world record in the 100 meters (1930) of 10.3 seconds - it stood for 11 years. (*answer p.50*)

278. **Track:** They called him "The Flying Finn" or "The Ace of Abo". What was his name? (*answer p.190*)

279. **Football:** _____ was voted the Jim Thorpe Trophy in 1957 by the NFL players. (*answer p.62.*)

280. **Soccer:** His nickname was "Kaiser Franz". What was his rightful name? (*answer p.134*)

JACKIE ROBINSON

281. **Hockey:** He won the NHL scoring championship 6 times, the Most Valuable Player award 6 times and was chosen for the All-Star team 9 times. (***answer p.136)***

282. **Boxing:** Actors Ruby Keeler, Al Jolson and George Raft bought his contract in the mid 30's for $10,000 - and put him on the road to success. Who was this Hollywood protege? (***answer p.148)***

283. **Boxing:** _____ won the American light heavyweight title by defeating Battling Levinsky in 1922. (***answer p.24)***

284. **Baseball:** In 1972, 25 years after his death, this home run king was admitted to baseball's Hall of Fame. (***answer p.198)***

285. **Swimming:** Winner of a bronze in 1928, he was an Olympic gold medalist (1932) in the 400-meter freestyle. (***answer p.160)***

286. **Football:** In 1946 he refused an offer of $25,000 a year - highest ever to that time - to play for the Chicago Rockets in the new All-American Conference. (***answer p.112)***

287. **Basketball:** _____ came out of retirement (1969-70) to sign as player-coach of the Cincinnati Royals. (***answer p.164)***

288. **Jockeys:** _____ holds the record for most wins ... 8,832 over 40 years. (***answer p.58)***

289. **Boxing:** John L. Sullivan called him "a fighting machine on stilts". To whom was he referring? (***answer p.80)***

290. **Golf:** At the age of 55, in the 1967 Masters tournament, he scored a record 30 on the back nine. (***answer p.84)***

WILLIE SHOEMAKER

291. **Figure Skating:** At the age of 15, she won (1964) the US Senior Ladies Championship - the youngest ever to do so. (*answer p.128*)

292. **Baseball:** In 1986, _____ reached a total of 4,256 hits - surpassing Ty Cobb's long-standing record of 4,191. (*answer p.22*)

293. **Tennis:** He organized his first tour (1953), playing a series of international matches against Australia's Frank Sedgeman. (*answer p.16*)

294. **Football:** He was known in the Canadian Football League as "Old Spaghetti Legs". What was his name? (*answer p.70*)

295. **Baseball:** _____ won the Rookie of the Year Award in 1947, playing for the pennant-winning Brooklyn Dodgers. (*answer p.56*)

296. **Jockeys:** Born in 1916, this jockey was a 5 time Kentucky Derby winner, won 6 Preakness Stakes and 6 Belmont Stakes. (*answer p.152*)

297. **Hockey:** Born (1929) in Winnipeg, this goalkeeper holds the shutout record of 12 in a single season - but did it 3 times. (*answer p.76*)

298. **Football:** This ex-Saskatchewan quarterback and coach became a CBC sports commentator in 1982. (*answer p.88*)

299. **Baseball:** Two of his brothers, Vince and Dominic, also became big league ball players. (*answer p.144*)

300. **Hockey:** In 1950, _____ was chosen Canada's all-round athlete of the half century. (*answer p.158*)

HELEN
WILLS
MOODY

301. **Soccer:** Before signing a professional contract (1964) with Bayern, he was an insurance salesman, worked in a clothing store. (*answer p.134*)

302. **Baseball:** Pitching for Miami, this 50 year-old right-hander's record was 11-4, his earned-run average an astounding 1.86. (*answer p.68*)

303. **Hockey:** His shot traveled over 120 miles per hour - the fastest ever recorded. Who was this left-winger? (*answer p.178*)

304. **Basketball:** Born (1936) in Philadelphia, this superstar was jumping 6 ft. 7 in. and running the 440 yds. in 49 seconds - as a teenager. (*answer p.188*)

305. **Football:** "I'm going to break all your records", he told Jim Brown. _____ did, in fact, break some of them. (*answer p.120*)

306. **Baseball:** The first black player in the International League, _____ led the Montreal Royals to the IL pennant in 1946. (*answer p.56*)

307. **Boxing:** Taking refuge behind the color bar, Jack Dempsey refused several times to meet this outstanding black challenger. He was _____? (*answer p.64*)

308. **Hockey:** Over 32 years of major league play, he scored a record 975 goals and 1,383 assists. Who did it? (*answer p.136*)

309. **Tennis:** From the age of 16 to 29 this French champion remained unbeaten. What was her name? (*answer p.142*)

310. **Baseball:** When the baseball Hall of Fame was established, _____ received more votes for admission than any other player. (*answer p.12*)

JOHNNY
UNITAS

311. Track: A four-time US champion in the 1,500 meters, he became director of athletics at Cornell U. in 1938. (*answer p.154*)

312. Swimming: At the age of 18, holder of 35 world records, he won 2 golds, a silver and a bronze in the 1968 Mexico City games. (*answer p.192*)

313. Soccer: When he was 14, Sao Paolo turned him down as too young. Later they offered him - unsuccessfully - $500,000 to join them. (*answer p.66*)

314. Swimming: In a poll of Associateu Press sportswriters (1950), _____ was voted the Swimmer of The Half-Century. (*answer p.86*)

315. Boxing: _____ took the heavyweight title away from Tommy Burns (1908) in a bout in Sydney, Australia - his purse was $5,000. (*answer p.90*)

316. Figure Skating: In the 1964 Innsbruck (Austria) Olympics, this 15 year-old American finished 6th - it was her 1st international competition. She was? (*answer p.128*)

317. Baseball: He beat the Yankees in the 2nd and 6th games of the 1926 World Series. In the 7th game, he struck out Tony Lazzari to win the game and series. (*answer p.156*)

318. Tennis: In 1949 she became a staff sports announcer for WNEW, New York, often predicting the results of .... college football games. (*answer p.38*)

319. Boxing: Weighing only 151 lbs he lost a 15-round decision to future heavyweight champion Jack Johnson, who later refused to meet _____ again. (*answer p.64*)

320. Soccer: After retiring as a player in 1973, he became manager of Preston North End. (*answer p.78*)

SAM LANGFORD

321. **Swimming:** His hometown of Lake Oswego, Ore. awarded him $1000 as a gesture of appreciation after his victories in the 1964 Tokyo Olympics. (*answer p.54*)

322. **Basketball:** _____ was named the NBA's Most Valuable Player after scoring a league-leading total of 2,596 points (1970-71). (*answer p.40*)

323. **Football:** Born 1932 in Knoxville, Tenn. this quarterback won the CFL West's Jeff Nicklin Trophy (most valuable player) 7 times between 1956 and 1964. (*answer p.70*)

324. **Hockey:** Born in Shawinigan Falls, Quebec (1929), this goalkeeper, over 23 years, played on 6 Stanley Cup winners, and 8 first place NHL Teams. (*answer p.186*)

325. **Baseball:** For 6 consecutive seasons this Nebraska-born hurler's earned-run average did not exceed 1.91. Who was this NL pitcher know as "Pete"? (*answer p.156*)

326. **Boxing:** In 1934 he lost his welterweight crown to Barney Ross in a split decision. (*answer p.48*)

327. **Football:** Before joining Saskatchewan (1963), he taught school in England, wrote radio and TV scripts. Who was this writing Roughrider?(*answer p.130*)

328. **Jockeys:** In 1987 _____ was sentenced to 3 years in prison for income tax evasion of more than $7 million. (*answer p.98*)

329. **Track:** This Canadian marathon champion was forced to drop out of the 1908 Olympic marathon after 19 miles. He was _____? (*answer p.126*)

330. **Boxing:** He was born in Cornwall, England in 1864. When he was 9, the family of this future heavyweight champion moved to New Zealand. (*answer p.80*)

PELE

331. **Tennis:** In her short pro career (late 50's), she earned more than $200,000 - sometimes in half-time exhibition matches during Harlem Globetrotter games. (*answer p.4*)

332. **Boxing:** This ex-heavyweight champion owns a 50-acre farm in Virginia - and is a zealous advocate of the Moslem religion. (*answer p.162*)

333. **Boxing:** He starred in a play written for him entitled The Honest Blacksmith, actually making horseshoes on stage. Who was this hammering heavyweight? (*answer p.80*)

334. **Baseball:** Considered by many, including John McGraw, as baseball's greatest all-rounder, his salary never exceeded $10,000 (1897-1917). (*answer p.122*)

335. **Tennis:** After losing in the Australian singles championship 5 times in a row, he finally captured it in 1960. (*answer p.146*)

336. **Basketball:** During this center's year (1961-62) with the Harlem Globetrotters, they won 411 games without a loss. (*answer p.188*)

337. **Jockeys:** Over 40 years (1927-1967) he rode in 32,402 races. Who was this veteran rider ? (*answer p.18*)

338. **Baseball:** Declaring himself a free agent in 1978 he left hometown Cincinnati for the Montreal Expos. Who was this free spirit? (*answer p.22*)

339. **Golf:** He tied for the lowest PGA single record score ever - 59. Who was this under-60? (*answer p.124*)

340. **Basketball:** He led the US collegiate leagues in 3 consecutive seasons, 1957-1959. (*answer p.138*)

SATCHEL PAIGE

341. Hockey: He signed for the Canadiens in 1923 but was so unsure of himself he returned his signing bonus. Who was this modest forward? (*answer p.114*)

342. Baseball: "I've found another Babe Ruth" .... that's how Yankee scout Paul Krichell described _____. (*answer p.184*)

343. Basketball: In 3 seasons with UCLA Bruins, this future Los Angeles Laker center led his team to a record of 88 games won, 2 lost and 3 consecutive NCAA championships. (*answer p.40*)

344. Tennis: Because of her cool, unflappable manner, she became known as "Little Miss Poker Face". What was her name? (*answer p.60*)

345. Golf: Between 1896 and 1914, he won the British Open 6 times, was 2nd four times. (*answer p.26*)

346. Jockeys: Through his career, _____ won 17 Triple Crown races - no one else had won more than 4. (*answer p.152*)

347. Track: He established a world record of 6:34 in the 1 1/2 mile distance (1937). (*answer p.154*)

348. Tennis: His first taste of success came in 1913 when he paired with Mary K. Browne to win the U.S. mixed doubles title. Mary's partner was _____? (*answer p.46*)

349. Baseball: With 23 wins against 7 losses (1924), _____ finally led the Washington Senators to a World Series victory. (*answer p.102*)

350. Tennis: In 1937, he captured both the Wimbledon and US championship. Who was this 22-year old? (*answer p.92*)

JACKIE PARKER

351. **Football:** This New York high school halfback chose Columbia despite other university athletic scholarships offers (1935) because he thought it to be academically superior. (*answer p.112)*

352. **Hockey:** After ending his hockey career in 1971, this ex-center became an executive in the front office of the Montreal Canadiens. (*answer p.174)*

353. **Tennis:** She was very influential in helping Althea Gibson break down the color bar which had long existed in big time tennis. Her name was _____? (*answer p.38)*

354. **Track:** A member of the Onandaga Indian Tribe, _____ first made his mark winning the Hamilton, Ontario round-the-bay race of 1906. (*answer p.126)*

355. **Boxing:** After winning his first 23 bouts, 19 by KO, he lost to Max Schmeling (1936) by a 12th round knockout. Who was this heavyweight? (*answer p.110)*

356. **Figure Skating:** Starting in 1927, _____ won the Women's Figure Skating Championship of the world for 10 consecutive years. (*answer p.74)*

357. **Basketball:** He became famous during the 50's by his ability to pass the ball behind his back without turning his head. (*answer p.164)*

358. **Golf:** He became famous for having invented "the reminder grip". Whom does this remind you of? (*answer p.6)*

359. **Football:** During his 16 years in the NFL, he completed 1,693 forward passes for 27,886 yards. (*answer p.182)*

360. **Hockey:** Although frequently referred to as "Mr. Hockey", "Mr. Elbows" would have been equally appropriate. (*answer p.136)*

FRED
PERRY

361. **Track:** In the 1924 Paris Olympics he won both the 1,500 and the 5,000 meters on the same day - never done before. (*answer p.190*)

362. **Hockey:** Born in 1887, he played goal for the local Chicoutimi, Quebec teams <u>without</u> skates up until 2 years before turning professional. (*answer p.34*)

363. **Baseball:** In his rookie year (1932), he won 18 games for the St. Louis Cardinals, mostly with his fastball. (*answer p.132*)

364. **Jockeys:** After graduating from high school, he tried to enlist in the US Air Force but was rejected as too short to pilot a plane (5 ft. 3 in.). (*answer p.168*)

365. **Football:** This ex-high school principal was fired as coach of the Toronto Argonauts (1976) when they finished last in the CFL Eastern conference. (*answer p.166*)

366. **Hockey:** Remembered chiefly as a hockey player, _____ was a member of the baseball Toronto Maple Leafs, winner of the AAA crown in 1926. (*answer p.158*)

367. **Tennis:** _____ sparked the formation of the Women's Tennis Association in opposition to the US Lawn Tennis Association. (*answer p.196*)

368. **Swimming:** He was no. 7 in the line of movie Tarzans. Who was he?(*answer p.160*)

369. **Tennis:** He defeated friend and mentor Gene Mako in 1933 to win his first national junior title, then teamed with him to win 2 national double crowns. (*answer p.92*)

370. **Soccer:** His nickname was "The Galloping Major". What was this soldier's name? (*answer p.106*)

SONJA HENIE

371. Hockey: When he was 18, still an amateur, his agent, Allen Eagleson, negotiated a 2-year $150,000 deal with the Boston Bruins for him. (*answer p.100)*

372. Boxing: After losing his heavyweight title he took a stab at wrestling, then bull-fighting, ended his career in NY's Hubert's Museum and Flea Circus. (*answer p.90)*

373. Football: Spotted as a future great in high school, he received scholarship offers from 52 universities - chose Alabama U. (*answer p.150)*

374. Swimming: Before he was 16 (1962), this North Carolina-born athlete had established 11 national age group records, 3 US freestyle records. (*answer p.54)*

375. Tennis: In 1963, this red-headed, 25-year old amateur champion turned professional - for a guaranteed $100,000 over 3 years. He was _____ ? (*answer p.146)*

376. Jockeys: In 1951, his 3rd year, he led the field in money-winning with $1.3 million. (*answer p.58)*

377. Figure Skating: _____ won 3 consecutive World Championships, in 1966-67-68. (*answer p.128)*

378. Boxing: He knocked out Sonny Liston to gain the world's heavyweight crown in 1964. (*answer p.162)*

379. Tennis: Born in Lancashire (1909), this future Wimbledon champion first developed as a table tennis champion. (*answer p.72)*

380. Tennis: In 1973, as an "amateur", _____ she earned more than $150,000, surpassing Billie Jean King's 1971 record. (*answer p.118)*

TERRY SAWCHUK

381. **Boxing:** Lightweight champion Georges Carpentier and middleweight champion Stanley Ketchell both refused him title fights by invoking the color bar. (*answer p.64*)

382. **Hockey:** Montreal novelist Hugh MacLennan said: " _____ was the greatest all-round forward the game has known." (*answer p.114*)

383. **Football:** This Illinois halfback was named to the All-American college team 3 years running: 1923, 1924, and 1925. (*answer p.140*)

384. **Baseball:** In 1952 the Milwaukee Braves purchased him from the Indianapolis Clowns for $2500 down, $7500 later. Who was this fantastic bargain? (*answer p.82*)

385. **Swimming:** Between 1921 and 1928, he set a record of 52 US national championship gold medals. Who was this collector of medals? (*answer p.86*)

386. **Tennis:** "The fox trot and shimmy are excellent training for tennis." What female champion offered this advice? (*answer p.142*)

387. **Football:** Turned down by Notre Dame and Indiana, this Pittsburgh-born grid star was finally accepted by the University of Louisville (1950). (*answer p.62*)

388. **Golf:** At the age of 50 and suffering from tuberculosis, he narrowly missed winning the USGA Open (1920). (*answer p.26*)

389. **Baseball:** After 3 years in the US Army, he joined the Kansas City Monarchs (1945) as shortstop at $400 a month. (*answer p.56*)

390. **Golf:** At the age of 21 (1923), he had won 13 major tournaments. Who was this legendary linkster? (*answer p.176*)

BOBBY
CHARLTON

391. Track: This future sprint champion worked as a night elevator operator for $150 a month to put himself through Ohio State U. in the mid 30's. (***answer p.104***)

392. Golf: The first player in a PGA event to shoot his own age, _____ shot a 67 (and a 66) in the 1979 Quad Cities Open. (***answer p.124***)

393. Football: "Off My Chest" was the title of his book written with Myron Cope, published in 1964. Whose autobiography was this? (***answer p.96***)

394. Basketball: _____ turned down over 200 offers from various universities to play under coach Forest "Phog" Allen at Kansas University (1954) - and a $15-a-week job. (***answer p.188***)

395. Baseball: Although no statistical records were kept in the Negro League, he was reliably reported to have hit 75 home runs in one season, 89 in another. (***answer p.198***)

396. Football: Graduating from Syracuse U., he was signed by the Cleveland Browns in 1957, won the NFL Rookie of the Year award. (***answer p.96***)

397. Basketball: He turned down many offers from various colleges (1957) to play under coach George Smith at the University of Cincinnati. (***answer p.138***)

398. Jockeys: His last winning race (1966) was his 6,032nd victory - a record to that date. He was _____? (***answer p.18***)

399. Baseball: _____ set a modern National League record of 37 wins against 11 losses in 1908. (***answer p.2***)

400. Boxing: While holding the welterweight title, _____ won the world middleweight title from Jake La Motta by a K.O. (1951). (***answer p.36***)

BOB FITZSIMMONS

401. Soccer: At the age of 15, he was spotted in Belfast by Bob Bishop, scout for Manchester United (1961). (*answer p.200*)

402. Football: Between 1956 and 1974 this quarterback was voted the NFL's Most Valuable Player 3 times, played in 10 Pro Bowl games. (*answer p.62*)

403. Jockeys: The names of his 5 Kentucky Derby winners were: Iron Liege, Venetian Way, Decidedly, Northern Dancer and Roart. Who rode them? (*answer p.168*)

404. Boxing: Though down for the "long count", he still was able to retain his heavyweight title in a 1927 re-match. (*answer p.24*)

405. Hockey: Offered the coaching job of the Montreal Canadiens (1936), Cecil Hart accepted .... on the condition that Chicago's _____ be brought back to Montreal. (*answer p.114*)

406. Football: Over 13 years (1963-1976), he scored a CFL record of 137 touchdowns, 46 more than his closest rival. Who was he? (*answer p.130*)

407. Soccer: Joining Real Madrid, _____ earned over 250,000 pounds became Spain's leading scorer 1959 through 1964. (*answer p.106*)

408. Baseball: Brought up from the age of 8 in a Baltimore school for incorrigible boys, this future Yankee learned to play baseball there. (*answer p.44*)

409. Hockey: Recruited by Vancouver in 1911, he was paid $5,260 a year - the most ever for a hockey player till then. (*answer p.52*)

410. Baseball: He was considered the most unpopular big leaguer of his time .... and perhaps the best. Who was this 20th century Tiger? (*answer p.12*)

HENRY AARON

411. Baseball: In a much-publicized exhibition game (1930) against a white major league barn-storming team, he struck out 22 in 1 game. (*answer p.68*)

412. Baseball: In 13 consecutive seasons (1925-38) Yankee _____ drove in more than 100 runs and himself scored more than 100 runs. (*answer p.184*)

413. Hockey: _____ was such a sensation with the Quebec Citadelles in 1947-49, it was necessary to build a larger arena to accommodate the fans. (*answer p.174.*)

414. Football: When his career ended in 1980, _____ had chalked up 11,236 yards, 2nd highest-ever NFL total. (*answer p.120*)

415. Baseball: An unrepentant racist, this Detroit Tiger was once sued by a black chambermaid whom he assaulted when she resented his calling her "nigger". (*answer p.12*)

416. Soccer: Born in 1915, he became a professional with Stoke City at 17 -- at 5 pounds per week and 10 pound bonus. (*answer p.42*)

417. Hockey: His suspension for striking a referee in Montreal (1955) led to one of the worst riots in Canadian history. (*answer p.14*)

418. Golf: He captured the US Open twice and the PGA championship a record 5 times. (*answer p.20*)

419. Boxing: After World War I, he was billed as "The Fighting Marine". Officially he was known as _____? (*answer p.24*)

420. Basketball: This 7 ft. 2 in. center was such a sensation in high school that over 200 US colleges competed for his services - UCLA got him (1965). He was _____? (*answer p.40*)

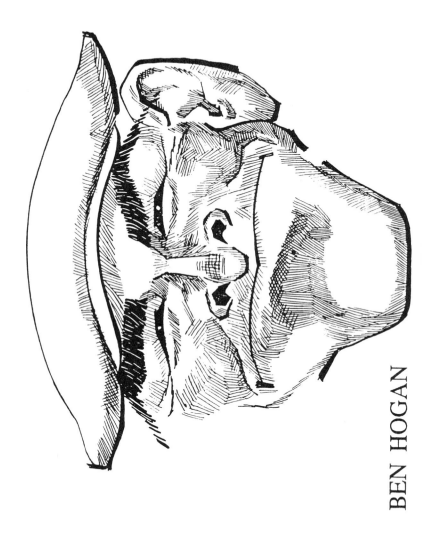

BEN HOGAN

421. **Track:** In 1924, he won the 1,500 meters in 3:52.6. Forty-five minutes later, he captured the 5,000 meters in 14:28.2 -- both were world records. (**answer p.190**)

422. **Football:** In 1975, he became the head coach of the Toronto Argonauts, the first CFL Canadian coach since 1949. Who was he? (**answer p.166**)

423. **Baseball:** In 8,399 official times at bat, he averaged a record 1 home run in every 11.7 times. (**answer p.44**)

424. **Track:** Because it was a paced race, his fastest-ever 4:04.4 mile was not recognized as a record (1938). Who was the unrecognized miler? (**answer p.154**)

425. **Boxing:** In 1897, he fought Jim Corbett in Carson City, Nevada for the heavyweight championship. _____ won by a KO in the 14th round.(**answer p.80**)

426. **Tennis:** In 1970, _____ achieved the Grand Slam, winning the Australian, French, British and US open titles - a feat achieved before only by Maureen Connolly. (**answer p.118**)

427. **Track:** Though considered the world's best distance runner, his contract with the Irish-Canadian AC was sold for $2000 in 1909. (**answer p.126**)

428. **Soccer:** His West German team lost to England in the 1966 European championship but _____ led them to a reverse decision in 1972.(**answer p.134**)

429. **Hockey:** After a severe facial injury, he adopted a face mask - the first NHL goalie to do so. Who was this masked marvel? (**answer p.186**)

430. **Jockeys:** His last winner, in his last race was named George Royal (1967). What was the jockey's name? (**answer p.18**)

JOHNNY
WEISSMULLER

431. **Hockey:** The pro Montreal Canadiens discovered him in a match (1910) against an amateur Chicoutimi, Quebec team - Chicoutimi won 2-0. Who was in their goal? (*answer p.34*)

432. **Boxing:** His fight with French champion Georges Carpentier was the first million dollar gate in ring history. He won in 4 rounds (1921). (*answer p.108*)

433. **Soccer:** One year after he joined a very mediocre Valencia team they won the Spanish league championship, the first time in 24 years. (*answer p.116*)

434. **Swimming:** He starred in the _____ Aquaparade in the New York World's Fair. (*answer p.160*)

435. **Figure Skating:** At 16 (1945), she became the youngest skater to ever win the North American championship. (*answer p.28*)

436. **Track:** Though he made his reputation as an Olympic star, he later played for 3 major league baseball teams (1913-19). (*answer p.30*)

437. **Football:** He made a successful (at the box office) film called "One Minute to Play". Who was this halfback? (*answer p.140*)

438. **Jockeys:** He won his first race at the age of 12 (1947) on a horse called The Chase at Haddock Park, England. (*answer p.98*)

439. **Basketball:** This Boston Celtic guard averaged 18.4 points per game in his 13 year career and was in the top 10 NBA scorers 8 times.(*answer p.164*)

440. **Tennis:** In 1948 he captured the US professional championship. Who defeated Bobby Riggs? (*answer p.16*)

RON LANCASTER

441. **Baseball:** At the age of 59, the oldest player ever in the big leagues, _____ pitched 3 scoreless innings against the Boston Red Sox.(*answer p.68)*

442. **Soccer:** A Manchester star, he declared: "I know I burn the candle at both ends - if I'd been born ugly, you'd never have heard of Pele".(*answer p.200)*

443. **Baseball:** From 1925 to 1939 _____ played 2,130 consecutive games for the NY Yankees. (*answer p.184*)

444. **Football:** This Saskatchewan Roughrider holds the CFL record of 288 games played, 88 consecutively. (*answer p.88)*

445. **Baseball:** Born 1931 in Fairfield, Alabama he learned his baseball on his father's steel mill team. Who was this future NY Giant star? (*answer p.170)*

446. **Baseball:** In 1929, this ex-pitcher was named manager of the Washington Senators - lasting 4 years. (*answer p.102)*

447. **Football:** In 1940, this passer was the NFL's best punter averaging 51.4 yards. His lifetime average was 45.1 yards, a record. (*answer p.182)*

448. **Golf:** Independent record-keepers list him as having won 135 tournament victories - he claims 165. (*answer p.124.)*

449. **Baseball:** Magnavox paid him $250,000 a year to endorse their product - he also did commercials for O Henry candy bars. What player made these sweet deals? (*answer p.82)*

450. **Tennis:** She was the first Australian woman to win the US Open title in 1962 beating Darlene Hard. What was this Aussie star's name?(*answer p.118)*

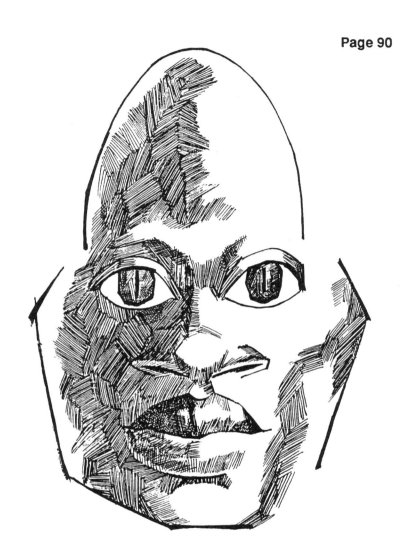

JACK JOHNSON

451. Baseball: He and his brother Paul each won 2 games in the Cardinals' defeat of Detroit in the 1934 World Series. (*answer p.132*)

452. Boxing: His boxing career began in 1899 when he knocked out a professional circus boxer in one round, earning $5. (*answer p.180*)

453. Track: He was barred from competing in his 4th Olympics (1932) on the grounds that he had accepted too many gifts to be still ranked an amateur. (*answer p.190*)

454. Baseball: In the early 40's this ex-Phillie was a sideshow attraction in a Times Square flea circus. Who was the Hall of Fame pitcher? (*answer p.156*)

455. Soccer: Stoke City traded him to Blackpool - where he owned a hotel - in 1947 for a bargain of 11,500 pounds. Who was this hotelier? (*answer p.42*)

456. Swimming: This American swimmer set a record (1921) for the 100-yard freestyle which stood for 22 years. (*answer p.86*)

457. Tennis: The title of her autobiography was "I Always Wanted To Be Somebody". Who was this author? (*answer p.4*)

458. Boxing: _____ was named (1950) Canada's boxer of the half-century in a Canadian press poll. (*answer p.48*)

459. Football: What Chicago Bear quarterback served in the World War II U.S. Merchant Marine, retired from football in 1950 and was inducted into The Hall of Fame 15 years later?(*answer p.112*)

460. Hockey: This goalie won the Rookie of the Year award in the US Hockey League, the American Hockey League and the NHL in 3 consecutive years (1948-51). (*answer p.76*)

DON
BUDGE

461. **Soccer:** "I got at least 1,500 goals but who's counting?" Who made this claim? (***answer p.106***)

462. **Tennis:** At 18 he came into international prominence by winning the US and Canadian junior championships (1956). (***answer p.146***)

463. **Boxing:** In 1927, _____ lost his heavyweight title to an ex-Marine before the largest crowd in the history of the ring, 120,757. (***answer p.108***)

464. **Basketball:** Thanks to this Milwaukee Buck's class action suit (1970), pro basketball's option clause and college draft rights were eliminated. Who was this litigant? (***answer p.138***)

465. **Baseball:** It was often said that the 3 most famous Americans in history were George Washington, Abraham Lincoln and _____. (***answer p.44***)

466. **Track:** Born in Danville, Ala. (1913), this future Olympic champion was already working in the cotton fields at the age of 6. (***answer p.104***)

467. **Football:** This famous all-American college halfback joined the pro Chicago Bears in 1925. (***answer p.140***)

468. **Boxing:** In France (1888), he fought to a 39-round draw with English heavyweight Charlie Mitchell - they were then arrested by police. (***answer p.172***)

469. **Tennis:** Bobby Riggs offered her $10,000 to play a match against him. She lost (1973). Who was she? (***answer p.118***)

470. **Boxing:** He turned pro as a welterweight in 1940, won 20 consecutive bouts, then defeated former champion Fritzie Zivic. (***answer p.36***)

BOB FELLER

471. **Baseball:** This Boston Red Sox left fielder won the AL batting championship 6 times, the MVP award twice (1946 and 1949). (***answer p.32)***

472. **Swimming:** He became the first swimmer to win 4 individual AAV titles in 1 meet (1971), including 3 world records. (***answer p.192)***

473. **Boxing:** He is the only fighter in boxing history to have won the heavyweight championship 3 times. Who was this 3-time title-holder? (***answer p.162)***

474. **Hockey:** As player-coach of the Winnipeg Jets (1975), _____ he notched the highest-ever major league total of 77 goals. (***answer p.178)***

475. **Jockeys:** In 1956 he won the famous Triple Crown and had the most winners in the US (347). Who was this easy rider? (***answer p.168)***

476. **Boxing:** In a 1938 rematch _____ he KO'd the German heavyweight champion in the first round. (***answer p.110)***

477. **Baseball:** He led the NL in shutouts 7 times, wins 6 times, strikeouts 6 times, earned-run average 5 times between 1911 and 1930. (***answer p.156)***

478. **Track:** Sprinter _____ was voted Canada's track and field athlete of the first half of the 20th century. (***answer p.50)***

479. **Boxing:** Ex-champion James Jeffries came out of retirement to challenge him - and lose by a KO in 1910 to _____? (***answer p.90)***

480. **Baseball:** He broke into the majors as a 2nd baseman (1963) - then played left field, later right field, 3rd base and finally 1st base. (***answer p.22)***

JIM BROWN

481. **Jockeys:** Because of his reserved manner, he became known as "Silent Shoe". What was the rest of his name? (*answer p.58*)

482. **Soccer:** Though his Dutch national team lost to W. Germany in the World Cup final, he was named the Most Valuable Player for 1974. Who was he? (*answer p.10*)

483. **Basketball:** He was drafted by the Milwaukee Bucks in 1969 for $1.4 million - signed a 5 year $1.2 million per year contract. (*answer p.40*)

484. **Boxing:** Having earned over $1/2 million, this Vancouver welterweight retired in 1936 at the age of 29. (*answer p.48*)

485. **Baseball:** In the mid-70's this Cincinnati Red was the first "singles hitter" to reach the $100,000 annual salary level. Who was he? (*answer p.22*)

486. **Boxing:** Standing only 5 ft. 7 in. tall, with a 84-in. reach this Nova Scotia native is ranked by Ring magazine as one of the 10 all-time great heavyweights. (*answer p.64*)

487. **Basketball:** Known as "Mr. Basketball" during his NBA career, he accepted the job of commissioner of the American Soccer League in 1974.(*answer p.164*)

488. **Jockeys:** He retired at age 50 (1985) after winning 4,349 races all over the world. (*answer p.98*)

489. **Football:** In 1973, this Buffalo Bill became the first NFL player to gain over 2,000 yards in 1 season. (*answer p.120*)

490. **Baseball:** In 1906, his first season, this Georgia-born outfielder won the AL batting championship. (*answer p.12*)

LESTER PIGGOTT

491. **Tennis:** She met a great French champion only once (1924), lost 6-3, 8-6. Who was this US loser? (***answer p.60)***

492. **Hockey:** Though he made his name with the Canadiens, he earlier turned down their offer, staying with his original team. Who was this Ace from Quebec? (***answer p.174)***

493. **Swimming:** A lifelong believer in physical fitness, he wrote an arthritis exercise book, appeared on TV fitness programs. (***answer p.160)***

494. **Swimming:** After his Olympic victories, _____ was named the 1972 Sullivan Award winner and World Swimmer of the Year. (***answer p.192)***

495. **Baseball:** _____ was the first baseball player to incorporate himself under the name of Ro-Fel, Inc. What was his name? (***answer p.94)***

496. **Track:** He was a surprise winner of the Boston Marathon of 1907, setting a record not broken till the course was made easier. (***answer p.126)***

497. **Hockey:** After leaving the Boston Bruins, he became general manager and coach of the Quebec Nordiques in 1973. (***answer p.186)***

498. **Tennis:** In "the battle of the sexes" (1973) she convincingly defeated ex-champion Bobby Riggs. Who was she? (***answer p.196)***

499. **Figure Skating:** In her first try, aged 18, she won the World Championship in 1947, repeated in 1948. (***answer p.28)***

500. **Football:** This Ottawa Roughrider rookie demanded and got a $500 bonus, a $4,500 contract and a weekly plane trip to Toronto for signing (1958). (***answer p.166)***

BOBBY ORR

501. Swimming: On June 5, 1927 at Ann Arbor, Michigan, he set 3 world records in the same day in the 100 yard, 200 meter and 220 yard events. (*answer p.86*)

502. Track: He is the only track star and football player to have a town named after him - it was formerly Mauch Chunk, Pa. What's it called now? (*answer p.30*)

503. Golf: Born on the Isle of Jersey (1870), _____ became famous for his costume of cap, plus fours and jacket, which he always wore. (*answer p.26*)

504. Hockey: The first NHL goal on a penalty shot in the Stanley Cup play-offs was scored (1968) on this Los Angeles Kings' goaltender. (*answer p.76*)

505. Tennis: In 5 seasons (1936-40) she won 18 championships at Wimbledon. She was ? (*answer p.38*)

506. Football: Ottawa Roughriders traded him (1963) for $500 to the team he then played for over 19 years. (*answer p.88*)

507. Boxing: Novelist Jack London sparked a racist campaign for a "White Hope" to defeat this heavyweight champion. (*answer p.90*)

508. Hockey: _____ moved from Chicago to Winnipeg in the newly-formed World Hockey Ass'n in 1972 - for $2 million. (*answer p.178*)

509. Track: After his 1928 Olympic sprint victories he was called "the greatest sprinter the world has ever seen" by Gen. Douglas MacArthur. Of whom was he speaking? (*answer p.50*)

510. Jockeys: _____ retired in 1961 with a record of 4,779 winners. (*answer p.152*)

WALTER JOHNSON

511. **Baseball:** He began to work in a Pennsylvania coal mine at age 12 (1886) at $3.50 per week, later increased this by playing semi-pro ball. (***answer p.122***)

512. **Hockey:** First dubbed "The Tornado", he later became "The Whirlwind" but is famous as "Cyclone". What was his surname? (***answer p.52***)

513. **Soccer:** In 1988 he signed a 1 year contract to coach Barcelona - at $250,000. What's the name of this high-priced Dutch coach? (***answer p.10***)

514. **Swimming:** At the age of 63, in 1971, he set a world age group record in the 400 meter freestyle. Who was this senior swimmer? (***answer p.160***)

515. **Football:** On a day named to honor him in 1943, this Brooklyner threw a record 7 touchdown passes to trample the NY Giants 56 to 7. (***answer p.112***)

516. **Golf:** At the age of 13 (1903), this future golf giant climbed out of his classroom window, never to return. Who was this artful dodger? (***answer p.20***)

517. **Figure Skating:** The International Olympic Committee threatened to revoke her amateur standing if she accepted a yellow convertible from her hometown Ottawa fans. (***answer p.28***)

518. **Baseball:** During the years 1903-1905, this NY Giant won 30, 33 and 31 games - a record equaled by only 1 other pitcher since 1900.
(***answer p.2***)

519. **Soccer:** Born in Brazil (1940), he quit school at 10, started playing with construction workers' teams. (***answer p.66***)

520. **Golf:** When he was 12 years old (1914), he shot a 70 to tie the record of an Atlanta, Georgia golf course. (***answer p.176***)

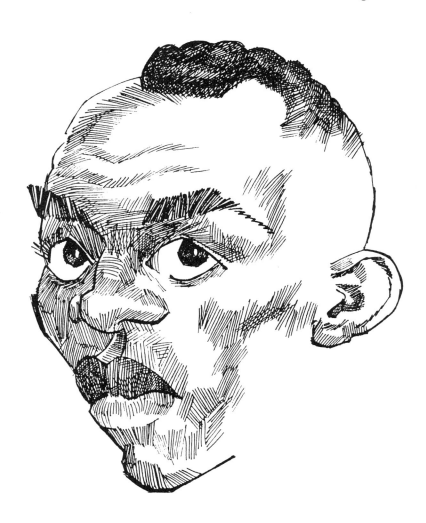

JESSE OWENS

Page 105

521. **Football:** As a rookie, he was cut by the Pittsburgh Steelers (1955) without playing in a single game. Who was this unappreciated quarterback? (*answer p.62*)

522. **Golf:** With James Braid and J. H. Taylor, he made up the famous "Great Triumvirate" which dominated golf at the turn of the century. (*answer p.26*)

523. **Tennis:** His Australian coach, Harry Hopman, nicknamed him "The Rocket". Who was this court comet? (*answer p.146*)

524. **Jockeys:** Among his many triumphs were the Ascot Gold Cup 3 times, the Epsom Derby 9 times and the St. Leger 8 times. (*answer p.98*)

525. **Boxing:** Because of his refusal to serve in the US Army during the war in Vietnam he was stripped of his heavyweight title in 1967. (*answer p.162*)

526. **Figure Skating:** She won the gold medal in figure skating in 3 consecutive Olympics: 1928, 1932 and 1936. Who was she? (*answer p.74*)

527. **Track:** Although Aldof Hitler refused to congratulate him on his triumphs in the Berlin Olympics (1936), _____ was a great hit with the German people. (*answer p.104*)

528. **Baseball:** This Cincinnati Red was voted by fans (1979) as the outstanding player of the decade. (*answer p.22*)

529. **Hockey:** This famous Montreal netminder was the father of 22 children. Who was this prolific father? (*answer p.34*)

530. **Basketball:** He led his San Francisco University team to 2 consecutive NCAA championships (1955-56) and a 60-game winning streak. (*answer p.8*)

FERENC PUSKAS

531. Baseball: Finishing with an average of .326, he was, at 40, the oldest player to capture a major league batting championship (1958).(*answer p.32)*

532. Baseball: Despite 2 years of military service (1952-54), this Giant outfielder stands 3rd on the all-time home run list (660). (*answer p.170)*

533. Boxing: He lost his heavyweight title in Sydney, Australia (1908) to the first black challenger for that title.   He was _____? (*answer p.180)*

534. Football: An unrivaled broken-field runner he was nicknamed "The Galloping Ghost" by Grantland Rice. What was his name? (*answer p.140)*

535. Tennis: "The most devastating and impressive player I have ever seen". Whom was Bobby Riggs describing? (*answer p.92)*

536. Hockey: Nov 19, 1952, _____ scored goal no. 325, making him the NHL's highest-ever scorer - the puck was sent to Queen Elizabeth. (*answer p.14)*

537. Baseball: Because of the speed of his pitches he became known as "The Big Train". What was his name? (*answer p.102)*

538. Swimming: A California high school student, _____ was the first person to swim the 200-meter freestyle in less than 2 minutes (1963). (*answer p.54)*

539. Soccer: This star became widely known as "The Wizard of Dribble". Who was he? (*answer p.42)*

540. Hockey: He became world-famous as "The Golden Jet". What was his name? (*answer p.178)*

JACK DEMPSEY

541. **Baseball:** In deep financial trouble, the Boston Red Sox sold him to the NY Yankees for more than $400,000 in 1919. Whom did they sell? (*answer p.44*)

542. **Boxing:** Bare-knuckle heavyweight fighting ended in 1889 - he was the last bare-knuckle champion. (*answer p.172*)

543. **Football:** This Cleveland Brown won the NFL's Most Valuable Player Award 3 times between 1957 and 1965. Who was this Brown? (*answer p.96*)

544. **Hockey:** In 1971 he played in an exhibition match with two of his own sons. Who was the proud father? (*answer p.136*)

545. **Baseball:** He won 3 major league Most Valuable Player awards in 1938, 1940 and 1947. Who was this triple threat? (*answer p.144*)

546. **Jockeys:** In his 2nd year of racing (1950), he tied for the US national championship with 388 wins. (*answer p.58*)

547. **Baseball:** Over 24 seasons his career batting average was .367, the highest in modern big league history. (*answer p.12*)

548. **Football:** For 2 seasons, he shared quarterback duties on the Ottawa Roughriders - till his rival was traded to Regina in 1962. (*answer p.166*)

549. **Tennis:** She turned professional in 1940 for $25,000 and a cut of gate receipts. (*answer p.38*)

550. **Hockey:** After scoring only 8 goals in the 1933-34 season, he was traded to the Chicago Blackhawks by the Montreal Canadiens. Who was this tradee? (*answer p.114*)

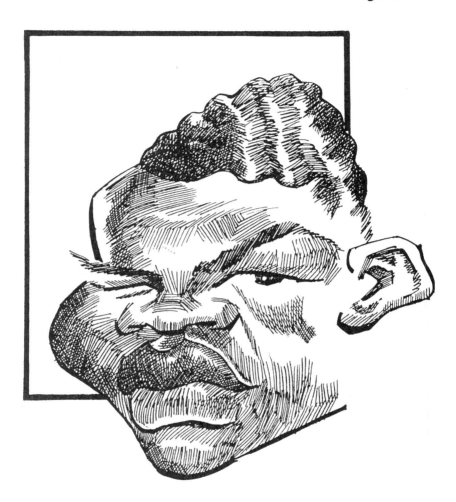

JOE LOUIS

551. **Track:** After he won the sprint double at Amsterdam in 1928, his diary entry read: "I'm supposed to be the world's 100m. champion. (Crushed apples.) No more fun in running now." (*answer p.50*)

552. **Baseball:** Dedicated to humanitarian causes this record home run hitter established a scholarship at Atlanta's Morris Brown University. (*answer p.82*)

553. **Boxing:** In 1903 he defeated ex-lightweight champion Joe Gans but he never won the title himself. (*answer p.64*)

554. **Football:** A member of Southern California University's track team, he anchored their 440-yd relay team (1967) to a world record. (*answer p.120*)

555. **Baseball:** In winning over 30 games in 3 consecutive seasons, _____ equalled Christy Matthewson's NL record. (*answer p.156*)

556. **Track:** He held the world mile record (4:06.7) for only 1 year (1936-7) when it was eclipsed by Sidney Wooderson of the UK. Whose record did Wooderson beat? (*answer p.154*)

557. **Tennis:** In 1938, she set a record of 8 Wimbledon Singles titles. Who was this US star? (*answer p.60*)

558. **Basketball:** He was "only" 6 ft. 5 in. tall. Who was known as the "Big O"? (*answer p.138*)

559. **Baseball:** _____ was signed by Cleveland Indians at the age of 42 (1948), the oldest rookie in baseball history. (*answer p.68*)

560. **Golf:** He won 3 Vardon Trophies, was the leading US money winner 4 times between 1940 and 1960. (*answer p.84*)

SID LUCKMAN

561. **Tennis:** In 1931, Henri Cochet of France defeated both him and Bunny Austin in the Davis Cup challenge round. (**answer p.72**)

562. **Boxing:** His given names were "William Harrison" but he (and 2 brothers) adopted the name "Jack", after a famous boxer of the time. What was his surname? (**answer p.108**)

563. **Baseball:** He broke into pro sports in football (1941) with the Los Angeles Bulldogs. Who was this future Brooklyn star? (**answer p.56**)

564. **Golf:** "The father of modern golf", never took a lesson, learned through caddying, starting at the age of 7 (1877). What was Papa's name? (**answer p.26**)

565. **Hockey:** As a defenseman over 11 years (1925-36), for Pittsburgh, Montreal and Chicago he suffered more than 600 stitches and 8 broken noses. (**answer p.158**)

566. **Tennis:** In 1934, she collapsed on a court in Paris, was diagnosed as having tuberculosis and might never be able to play again but _____ did. (**answer p.38**)

567. **Boxing:** By defeating champion Barney Ross, _____ won the world welterweight title in 1938. (**answer p.148**)

568. **Soccer:** Though he played for Hungary's army team and rose to the rank of major, he never carried a rifle. (**answer p.106**)

569. **Football:** In order to retain his athletic scholarship at Mississippi State, he and his wife were divorced in the early 50's - re-married a year later. (**answer p.70**)

570. **Baseball:** This Cleveland pitcher entered the US Navy in 1942, served on the USS alabama during World War 2. (**answer p.94**)

HOWIE MORENZ

571. **Basketball:** Bill Russell called him "the greatest player to play this game". To which Milwaukee Buck was he referring? (***answer p.40)***

572. **Boxing:** He won the light-heavyweight title at the age of 40 in 1904, lost it a year later. (***answer p.80)***

573. **Baseball:** Offered $20,000 by New York (double his Pittsburgh salary) this shortstop refused. Who was this nay player? (***answer p.122)***

574. **Tennis:** She was the first black woman to play in the US Nationals at Forest Hill (1950). What was her name? (***answer p.4)***

575. **Hockey:** As a "rover" and then a defenseman, he scored 17 goals in 21 games (a record), helping Ottawa win the Stanley Cup in 1909. (***answer p.52)***

576. **Jockeys:** He was once "traded" in Calgary, Alberta for a horse named Reddy Fox. (***answer p.18)***

577. **Track:** Turning professional in 1908, he won famous races in Madison Square Garden against Italian Dorando Pietri and Alfie Shrubb of the UK. (***answer p.126)***

578. **Soccer:** In 1964, _____ surprised the soccer world by moving from Real Madrid to Barcelona's Espanol. (***answer p.116)***

579. **Golf:** Unusually short for a top-notch golfer - not to say TV host, _____ was only 5 ft. 5 in. tall. (***answer p.6)***

580. **Hockey:** In 14 years of NHL play (1923-37) he scored a record 270 goals and 467 points. (***answer p.114)***

ALFREDO DI STEFANO

581. **Football:** The Baltimore Colts acquired his services (1956) from the semi-pro Bloomfield Rams for the price of a phone call. Who was this 80-cent bargain? (*answer p.62)*

582. **Tennis:** Turning professional at 38 _____ went on to win 340 out of 487 matches (1931-35). (*answer p.46)*

583. **Baseball:** From 1903 to 1915 this NY Giant pitcher never dropped under 22 wins per seasons. (*answer p.2)*

584. **Hockey:** In his first NHL season (1942-3), this Canadian right-winger broke his ankle so badly doctors advised him to give up the game. _____ didn't. (*answer p.14)*

585. **Boxing:** _____ lost his heavyweight title to Jess Willard in Havana, Cuba (1915) in the 26th round of a scheduled 45-round match. (*answer p.90)*

586. **Track:** "If I can keep one boy from smoking it will be worth more to me than all the money your firm could afford to pay." Who said this to a famous cigarette manufacturer? (*answer p.154)*

587. **Tennis:** Although she defeated Margaret Court at Wimbledon in 1961, it wasn't until 1965 that she defeated her again to win the women's singles title. (*answer p.196)*

588. **Hockey:** With Boston over 9 years, he won the Norris Trophy 8 years in a row, (1968-1975). (*answer p.100)*

589. **Baseball:** Despite 5 years of military service in 2 wars (World War II and Korea), _____ retired with a 521 homers total, 3rd highest in major league history till then. (*answer p.32*)

590. **Swimming:** He played both Flash Gordon and Buck Rogers in Hollywood "B" films. Who was this "B" actor? (*answer p.160)*

MARGARET COURT

591. **Figure Skating:** The world's most famous figure skater, she also won 18 skiing championships during the 30's and 40's. (*answer p.74*)

592. **Hockey:** Though he made his reputation in hockey, he also played Lacrosse for the Ottawa Capitals (1908-10). (*answer p.52*)

593. **Tennis:** Ex-champion Alice Marble helped this Harlem youngster to break big time tennis' color bar (1949). She was _____? (*answer p.4*)

594. **Boxing:** Triumphing over Tommy Bell in 1946, _____ became the world welterweight champion. (*answer p.36*)

595. **Golf:** At the age of 53, _____ won the $70,000 Greensboro Open (1965), the oldest player to win a PGA event. (*answer p.124*)

596. **Baseball:** His Yankee nickname was "The Iron Horse". Otherwise he was known as _____. (*answer p.184*)

597. **Soccer:** In 300 plus international games with his Santos team, they lost only once - to England. (*answer p.66*)

598. **Track:** After his 1936 Olympic victories, he returned home to become a disc jockey, a PR representative and a US good will ambassador. (*answer p.104*)

599. **Basketball:** Breaking into the NBA in 1959 with Philadelphia Warriors, _____ was the league's top scorer for 7 straight years.(*answer p.188*)

600. **Baseball:** This "bee ball" pitcher is famous for his maxim: "Don't look back. Something may be gaining on you." Who said it? (*answer p.68*)

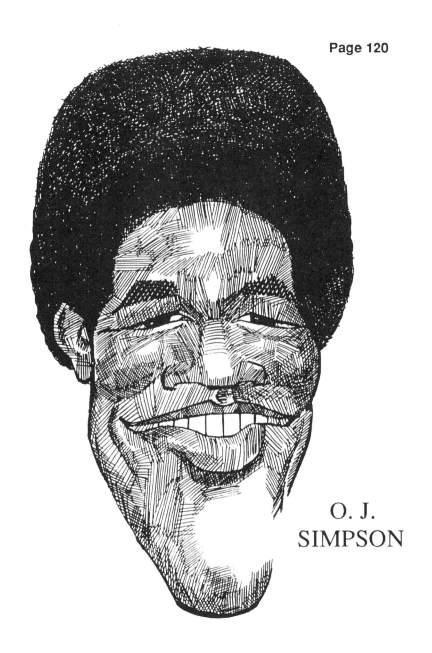

O. J.
SIMPSON

601. **Tennis:** _____ was the first American to win the men's singles title at Wimbledon (1920). (*answer p.46)*

602. **Boxing:** This heavyweight's first important professional bout was against Archie Moore, whom he kayoed in 4 rounds, as he'd predicted. (*answer p.162)*

603. **Baseball:** This shortstop began his pro career with Ed Barrow's Paterson, N.J. team (1895), was then sold to Louisville, Ky. in the National League (1897). (*answer p.122)*

604. **Swimming:** Previous to his Tokyo victories in 1964, only Jesse Owens had ever won 4 golds in an Olympiad. (*answer p.54*)

605. **Baseball:** His pitching talent was spotted by a traveling liquor salesman, who persuaded the Washington Senators to sign him (1907). (*answer p.102)*

606. **Hockey:** After prolonged knee problems, _____ announced his retirement (1979) from the Chicago Blackhawks to whom he'd been traded by Boston. (*answer p.100)*

607. **Boxing:** He defended his heavyweight title 25 times, scoring 21 KO's in the process. (*answer p.110)*

608. **Jockeys:** The horses he rode earned $30,039,543 over 31 years (1930-1961)—his share being roughly 10 percent. (*answer p.152*)

609. **Football:** _____ became (1963) the first ever to win both the CFL outstanding Canadian and the Schenley Trophy. (*answer p.166)*

610. **Figure Skating:** In 1948 her countrymen named her the outstanding living Norwegian. What was the lady's name? (*answer p.74)*

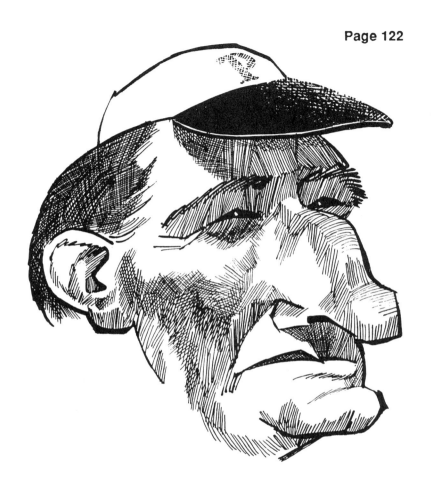

HONUS WAGNER

611. **Basketball:** The Boston Celtics were a cellar club when he joined them in 1953. They went on to win 6 NBA championships in 13 years. (*answer p.164*)

612. **Hockey:** A tragic crash, embedding his skate in the boards, ended his career - and his life - in 1937. (*answer p.114*)

613. **Boxing:** After retiring in 1940, he made a comeback in 1941 whipping Fritzie Zivic the 3rd time round but the middleweight title eluded him. (*answer p.148*)

614. **Soccer:** In 1929, he was selected for England's schoolboy team at 14 - they defeated Wales 4-1. He was _____? (*answer p.42*)

615. **Baseball:** In 1930, he became a regular on the Homestead Grays in the Negro League - and hit 75 home runs that year. (*answer p.198*)

616. **Hockey:** _____ himself denied a legend that he wagered that he would score a goal skating backwards for Renfrew against Ottawa (1911). (*answer p.52*)

617. **Baseball:** When he retired in 1951, the New York Yankees retired his uniform no. 5. (*answer p.144*)

618. **Golf:** This "hill-billy" holds the lowest stroke average for a year - 69.2 strokes through 96 rounds (1950). Name this "hill-billy". (*answer p.124*)

619. **Football:** Waived by all the NFL clubs (1955), this Pittsburgh native played semi-pro football for The Bloomfield Rams at $6 per game. (*answer p.62*)

620. **Basketball:** He led the US Olympic team to a 1960 gold medal, beating Brazil in the final 90-63. (*answer p.138*)

SAM SNEAD

621. **Tennis:** Born in 1943, she was twice ranked the world's no. 1 female tennis player and was named AP Athlete of the year in 1967 and 1973. (*answer p.196)*

622. **Baseball:** Born in Cairo, Georgia, this Brooklyn Dodger star retired in 1957 to work as an executive for the Chock Full O' Nuts fast-food chain. (*answer p.56)*

623. **Boxing:** Pushed back into the ring by newsmen after he'd been knocked through the ropes by Luis Firpo in the first round, he proceeded to win by a KO in the 2nd. (*answer p.108)*

624. **Hockey:** During a game against Pittsburgh (1925), he collapsed in the Montreal nets, was dead of TB 4 months later. (*answer p.34)*

625. **Football:** Buffalo Bills traded him (1978) to the San Francisco 49ers for 5 draft choices - at a salary of around $800,000 annually. Who was the tradee? (*answer p.120)*

626. **Baseball:** 23 years old (1941), _____ led the majors with a .406 batting average, the last player to top the .400 mark. (*answer p.32)*

627. **Tennis:** From 1933 to 1938 this ex-champion was director of a government-sponsored tennis school in Paris. Who was she? (*answer p.142)*

628. **Tennis:** "Retiring" in 1966, she married a wool broker and yachtsman named Smith in 1967. He persuaded _____ to get back in the game. (*answer p.118)*

629. **Soccer:** He and a famous Hungarian superstar played together on Real Madrid in the early 60's. Who was this Argentinian? (*answer p.116)*

630. **Boxing:** _____ was the only Canadian ever to hold the world heavyweight championship. (*answer p.180)*

TOM LONGBOAT

631. **Hockey:** This ex-Winnipegger holds the NHL shutout record of 103. His name was _____? (*answer p.76)*

632. **Boxing:** After losing his welterweight crown, he defeated ex-champions Tony Canzoneri and Lou Ambers in 1935-6, then retired. (*answer p.48)*

633. **Soccer:** In the 1968 European Cup final, he scored England's winner against Portugal's Benfica squad. The scorer was _____? (*answer p.78)*

634. **Basketball:** His scoring total in college basketball was 2,973, a record to that time (1959). He was _____? (*answer p.138)*

635. **Baseball:** Pitching for the Washington Senators over 20 years, _____ achieved an all-time strikeout record of 3,508 till Nolan Ryan broke it (1989).(*answer p.102*)

636. **Boxing:** 2 months after losing his crown to middleweight Randy Turpin, this ex-Detroiter won it back in a 10th round K.O. (1951). (*answer p.36)*

637. **Jockeys:** A sturdy, 4 ft. 11 in., wee Willie _____ won a 95-105 lb boxing crown in his Los Angeles high school. (*answer p.58)*

638. **Figure Skating:** At the age of 11 she captured the Canadian Junior title, the youngest ever to win it (1940). She was _____? (*answer p.28)*

639. **Baseball:** In his major league rookie year (1939), this Boston Red Sox outfielder hit .327, led the league with 145 RBI. (*answer p.32)*

640. **Tennis:** Between 1920 and 1929, he won 7 US singles championships, 6 of them consecutively. (*answer p.46)*

PEGGY FLEMING

641. **Hockey:** In his 18 year career (1942-1960) this right-winger played for 8 Stanley Cup winners and 8 first-place teams. (*answer p.14*)

642. **Football:** One of only two players to be so named 3 times, he was the CFL's most valuable player in 1957, 1958 and 1960. (*answer p.70*)

643. **Boxing:** In his heavyweight title defense in 1927, he earned $990,000 - the highest pay ever for a single athletic performance till then. (*answer p.24*)

644. **Basketball:** As a high school hoopster at Power Memorial in New York city, he registered a record 2,067 points, led his team to 71 consecutive victories (1962-65). (*answer p.40*)

645. **Track:** Two years after his Olympic victories, Vancouver's _____ tore a muscle in his left thigh which effectively ended his track career (1930). (*answer p.50*)

646. **Baseball:** As a left-handed pitcher between 1915 and 1918, he won 78, lost 40 for the Boston Red Sox, led the AL twice. (*answer p.44*)

647. **Hockey:** In 18 NHL seasons (1942-60) he was amongst the top scorers 15 times, led the league 4 times. Who was this Montrealer? (*answer p.14*)

648. **Hockey:** After his death in 1926, the NHL established a trophy to be awarded to each year's best goalkeeper. After whom is the trophy named? (*answer p.34*)

649. **Boxing:** He started his career at 22 (1902) as a lightweight, moved up through the welterweight and middleweight divisions to the heavyweight class. (*answer p.64*)

650. **Soccer:** Playing for W. Germany, he gained his first "cap" in 1966 against The Swedish national team - he was 19. (*answer p.134*)

GEORGE REED

651. Golf: In 1 year (1930), he won the "Grand Slam" of golf - The British Amateur, The British Open, the US Amateur and the US Open. (*answer p.176*)

652. Tennis: After he turned promoter (1953) he became known as "Big Daddy". Who was he? (*answer p.16*)

653. Hockey: This left-winger, more than anyone else, made popular the slap shot. Who wielded the curved stick? (*answer p.178*)

654. Soccer: He played for River Plate, Argentina for 3 years (1945-48), was once the league's leading scorer and played on 7 Argentine international squads. (*answer p.116*)

655. Golf: He won 4 US Opens, 2 PGA championships, 2 Masters, and a British Open - plus numerous other tournaments in a period of 15 years (1941-56). (*answer p.84*)

656. Baseball: Though he retired in 1917, he still led the NL in games played, times at bat, hits, singles, doubles and triples at the time of his death (1955). (*answer p.122*)

657. Football: Plagued by knee problems, _____ was forced to quit the NY Jets (1970). He then invested in 2 NY restaurants bearing his name. (*answer p.150*)

658. Hockey: He led the Toronto Argos to the Grey Cup in 1921, scoring 3 touchdowns. Who was this future hockey great? (*answer p.158*)

659. Basketball: Joining the US Olympic team in 1956, he sparked them to an 89-55 victory over the USSR ... and a gold medal. (*answer p.8*)

660. Boxing: His triumph in 1910 over ex-champion James Jeffries led to race riots in the US - 19 people were killed, 5000 arrested. (*answer p.90*)

DIZZY DEAN

661. **Soccer:** Some of his soccer wealth was invested in a sausage factory - which ground out no profit for Hungarian star _____. (**answer p.106**)

662. **Boxing:** He won the heavyweight title (1881), then toured, offering $1000 to anyone who could stay 4 rounds with him - he knocked out 59 men in a row in the first round. (**answer p.172**)

663. **Baseball:** In 1938 Branch Rickey sold him to the Chicago Cubs for $185,000 and 3 players in the "Sore Arm Deal". Whose arm was it? (**answer p.132**)

664. **Track:** As a football player he had a standing $1000 wager that he could gain 10 yards in 4 downs any time, any place. He never lost. (**answer p.30**)

665. **Baseball:** This Cleveland pitcher organized a team of major leaguers in 1946 to tour with a Negro league all-star team headed by Satchell Paige. (**answer p.94**)

666. **Hockey:** In his first 5 seasons (1950-55) with Detroit, he maintained a goals-against record of less than 2 per game. (**answer p.76**)

667. **Tennis:** He retired in 1939 after a pro tour with Don Budge, in which the latter won 3 games out of every 4. (**answer p.72**)

668. **Swimming:** Working for a swim suit company at $500 weekly, he was offered a screen test (1929) for the film role of Tarzan. (**answer p.86**)

669. **Jockeys:** Retired from riding in 1967, _____ is the only man to win The Kentucky Derby as both a jockey and trainer. (**answer p.18**)

670. **Baseball:** Cub manager Joe McCarthy, fed up with his pitcher's alcoholism, traded him in 1926 to the St. Louis Cardinals.(**answer p.156**)

FRANZ BECKENBAUER

671. **Football:** Refusing offers from 3 pro leagues, this ex-Ottawa quarterback returned to his primary vocation - education (1969 and again in 1976). (*answer p.166*)

672. **Hockey:** The Detroit Red Wings signed this right-winger at 18 for a $4000 bonus. What was him name? (*answer p.136*)

673. **Baseball:** In 1949, _____ was named the NL's Most Valuable Player, led the league in batting and stolen bases. (*answer p.56*)

674. **Track:** Because he played baseball for travel expenses, he was stripped of his medal by the International Olympic Committee. (*answer p.30*)

675. **Golf:** Famous for his accuracy this English champion was nicknamed "The Greyhound". The name on his birth certificate was _____? (*answer p.26*)

676. **Football:** As a Chicago Bear quarterback in the 40's, he was chosen All-Pro 5 times. Who was this all-star? (*answer p.112*)

677. **Golf:** He was offered a spot on the Philadelphia Phillies baseball team in 1914, turned it down for a golfing career. (*answer p.20*)

678. **Hockey:** He was the first defenseman to win the NHL scoring record (120 points) in 1970 - repeated in 1975. (*answer p.100*)

679. **Baseball:** In 1947 _____ won the Triple Crown (for batters) a 2nd time but the MVP award went to a famous Yankee star. (*answer p.32*)

680. **Track:** At one point in his 12-year career (1920-32), _____ held over 40 indoor and outdoor distance records. (*answer p.190*)

GORDIE HOWE

681. **Football:** In his first year in the new American Football League (1926), he played for a team called the New York Yankees. (*answer p.140*)

682. **Tennis:** In 1971 he earned a record $292,717, became the first pro to earn $1 million (in 9 years). Who was this court millionaire? (*answer p.146*)

683. **Tennis:** She was twice (1939-40) voted the US' most outstanding female athlete. Who was this court queen? (*answer p.38*)

684. **Track:** Growing up in Cleveland, this sprinter became known as "The Buckeye Bullet". What was his name? (*answer p.104*)

685. **Hockey:** This Canadien ace won the Hart Trophy as the NHL's most valuable player twice in succession, 3 times in all. (*answer p.114*)

686. **Baseball:** His hometown of Cincinnati has named a park after him. He bears the name of what flower? (*answer p.22*)

687. **Football:** In 1958, he led the Baltimore Colts to their first-ever NFL championship. What was this quarterback's name? (*answer p.62*)

688. **Soccer:** In 1969, he set a record by surpassing the mark of 1000 goals in world-class soccer. (*answer p.66*)

689. **Swimming:** This Californian eclipsed Paovo Nurmi's 1924 Olympic gold medal record of 5. Name this eclipsing medalist. (*answer p.192*)

690. **Jockeys:** _____ is the only jockey to have swept the Triple Crown since Eddie Arcaro in 1948. (*answer p.168*)

OSCAR ROBERTSON

691. Hockey: "It's practically impossible for anyone who knows him to have any ill feelings toward _____." To whom was Punch Imlach referring? (*answer p.174*)

692. Swimming: Despite his active movie career (some 175 films), he managed a chain of swim pools under his own name. What was it? (*answer p.160*)

693. Baseball: In the 1905 World Series against the Philadelphia Athletics, he hurled 3 shutouts in 6 days. Who was this pitching Giant? (*answer p.2*)

694. Figure Skating: Since retiring from amateur skating in 1969, she has done 8 TV specials. (*answer p.128*)

695. Hockey: Playing as a pro over 18 years (1906-1922), he never lost a tooth or acquired a scar ... playing 60 minutes a game. (*answer p.52*)

696. Tennis: In 1969, a panel of international tennis experts named _____ the greatest tennis player in history. (*answer p.46*)

697. Swimming: In a dispute over a $130 sports jacket that he photo-modelled, the US Amateur Athletic Union ordered an investigation of his amateur standing. (*answer p.54*)

698. Boxing: A white racist much of his life, this heavyweight later became an evangelist in Vancouver, B.C. Who was he? (*answer p.180*)

699. Jockeys: He won the UK Jockey's Championship 11 times, the last time in 1982. Who was this English rider? (*answer p.98*)

700. Boxing: He defeated champion Young Corbett III by a 1st round KO (1933) to win the world welterweight title. He was _____? (*answer p.48*)

RED GRANGE

701. **Football:** In 1937 this future Washington superstar signed a contract to play baseball for the St. Louis Cardinals. He was _____? (*answer p.182*)

702. **Track:** This 110 lb., 18 year old Vancouver sprinter burst into prominence (1925) by equaling the world 100-meter record of 10.6 seconds. (*answer p.50*)

703. **Soccer:** Because of his injuries in the Munich air crash of 1968, doctors despaired of his ever playing again. Inside-left _____ was back with his Manchester team in weeks. (*answer p.78*)

704. **Tennis:** "She was the greatest woman player who ever lived." Of whom was Helen Wills Moody speaking? (*answer p.142*)

705. **Hockey:** Spotted while playing in Oshawa at the age of 12, _____ was immediately put on the Boston Bruins' protected list (1960). (*answer p.100*)

706. **Football:** He was chosen (1979) by Pro Football Monthly as the US Player of the Decade. Name this 20th century Buffalo Bill. (*answer p.120*)

707. **Baseball:** Named manager of his club in 1917, he ran it for only 5 games. Who was this Pittsburgh star who disliked managing? (*answer p.122*)

708. **Boxing:** Well ahead in points in a try (1952) for Joey Maxim's light-heavyweight title, he - and the referee - collapsed because of heat exhaustion. (*answer p.36*)

709. **Tennis:** Turning professional in 1937, he toured with Ellsworth Vines, winning 29 of 61 matches. (*answer p.72.*)

710. **Track:** In 1935, he set a broad jump record of 26 ft. 8 1/4 in. at Ann Arbor, Michigan - it lasted for 25 years. Who was this bounder? (*answer p.104*)

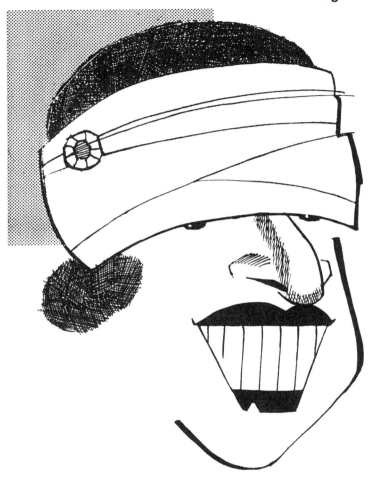

SUZANNE LENGLEN

711. **Tennis:** He won an under-15 tournament at the age of 8, but did not win the US national championship till he was 27 (1920) (*answer p.46*)

712. **Figure Skating:** In 1948, she swept the European, World and Olympic singles titles. Who was this new broom? (*answer p.28*)

713. **Golf:** He won the Atlanta Athletic Club's junior championship when he was 9 years old. Who was this youngster? (*answer p.176*)

714. **Baseball:** Over a career of 22 years, he led the NL in home runs 4 times with a high of 52 (1965) in San Francisco. (*answer p.170*)

715. **Boxing:** A fictionalized account of this heavyweight champion's life became an award-winning play and movie entitled "The Great White Hope". (*answer p.90*)

716. **Baseball:** This Phillie pitcher suffered from epilepsy yet remained effective on the mound (1911-1930). (*answer p.156*)

717. **Football:** Though not a critical success, this ex-NY Jet star made 4 movies plus a TV series, "The Waverly Wonders". (*answer p.150*)

718. **Track:** He first came to international prominence by winning the 1920 Olympic 10,000-meter and the 10,000-meter cross-country gold medals. (*answer p.190*)

719. **Golf:** Though he won every major tournament in pro golf, the US open title eluded him. No grand slam for _____? (*answer p.124*)

720. **Soccer:** His West German team won the World Cup in 1974. He was purchased by the NY Cosmos 3 years later. (*answer p.134*)

JOE
DI MAGGIO

721. **Football:** _____ set an NFL mark for TD passes in 47 straight games - a record up to 1960. (**answer p.62**)

722. **Figure Skating:** In 1924, at the ripe age of 11, she won the Norwegian women's figure-skating championship. What was this child's name? (**answer p.74**)

723. **Track:** His 1912 Olympic medals were returned to his family 70 years after they were officially taken away from _____. (**answer p.30**)

724. **Football:** Bob Zuppke, his famous Illinois college coach told him: "Football isn't meant to be played for money". Who was the advisee? (**answer p.140**)

725. **Hockey:** In the 1952 Stanley Cup play-offs this goalie registered 4 shutouts in 8 games. He was _____? (**answer p.76**)

726. **Tennis:** Wearing her famous eye-shade, American _____ won both the singles and doubles gold medals at the 1924 Olympics. (**answer p.60**)

727. **Track:** Although he held many middle distance records, he could finish no better than 2nd in the 1936 Olympic 1,500 meters race. (**answer p.154**)

728. **Jockeys:** His first win came in 1949 on a horse named Shafter V in his 3rd race. What was the rider's name? (**answer p.58**)

729. **Baseball:** _____ closed out his career with a major league record of 755 home runs. (**answer p.82**)

730. **Swimming:** He was a 16-letter man in high school in Honolulu, winning a letter every year in swimming, basketball, football and track. (**answer p.160**)

ROD LAVER

731. **Soccer:** He played 3 times for Blackpool in the FA cup final -- they finally won it in 1953. (*answer p.42*)

732. **Tennis:** Although recognized unanimously as the world's no. 1 player he had his nemesis ... Ken Rosewall who upset _____ several times. (*answer p.146*)

733. **Basketball:** Between 1950 and 1963 this Boston Celtic made the NBA all-star team every year. Who was he? (*answer p.164*)

734. **Hockey:** His Montreal team won the Stanley Cup in 1924. During the series _____ allowed only 6 goals in 6 games. (*answer p.34*)

735. **Soccer:** In 1944, he made his league debut in Hungary at the age of 16. (*answer p.106*)

736. **Baseball:** In 1949, _____ came out of an 8-year retirement to win the Manager of the Year award with the Washington Senators. (*answer p.32*)

737. **Football:** An outstanding player in the US Southeast Conference, he was offered a spot by the NY Yankees - he preferred football. Who was this Edmonton football-firster? (*answer p.70*)

738. **Soccer:** "Meet the player who will one day be the greatest in the world", said the Brazilian pro scout of his 15-year-old protege _____. (*answer p.66*)

739. **Tennis:** _____ competitive career ended in the 40's when one of her lungs was removed. (*answer p.38*)

740. **Boxing:** _____ celebrated his 21st birthday by knocking out England's Freddie Welsh (1917) to win the lightweight title. (*answer p.194*)

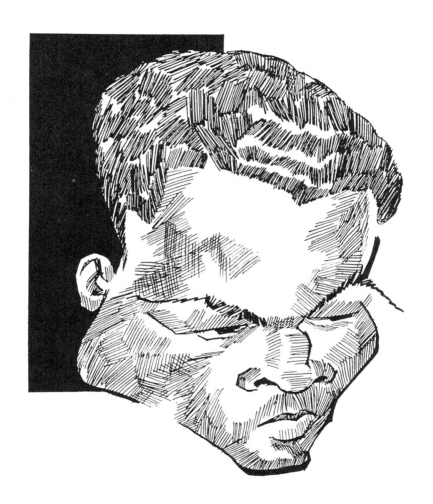

HENRY ARMSTRONG

741. **Hockey:** Captain of his Montreal team, no. 4's 509 goals and 712 assists were an all-time record for an NHL center. (*answer p.174*)

742. **Baseball:** Because of his energetic style of play he was nicknamed "Charlie Hustle". What was his true name? (*answer p.22*)

743. **Boxing:** His nickname, famous throughout the world was "The Manassa Mauler". Who was he? (*answer p.108*)

744. **Football:** This Chicago quarterback was named the NFL's Most Valuable Player in 1943. Who was this MVP? (*answer p.112*)

745. **Baseball:** Pitching for the Boston Red Sox farm team, he led the International League with a 22-9 record (1914). (*answer p.44*)

746. **Golf:** A bridge over the 15th hole of the Augusta National Golf course was named after him, 20 years after he won the Masters there. (*answer p.6*)

747. **Swimming:** There is a 6 ft. cement statue of _____ in the Swimming Hall of Fame, Ft. Lauderdale, Fla. (*answer p.192*)

748. **Football:** He guided his Alabama U. team to the US national championship in 1964. Who was this Pennsylvania-born quarterback? (*answer p.150*)

749. **Hockey:** Hockey's brightest star till 1922, he received only 1 advertising offer - to endorse underwear. (*answer p.52*)

750. **Baseball:** Born in Mobile, Alabama (1906), he earned his nickname by toting luggage at the local railway station. What was his name? (*answer p.68*)

JOE NAMATH

751. **Hockey:** His last NHL goal (1960) was a record 82nd in Stanley Cup play - and his career 626th. Who was this high flyer? (*answer p.14*)

752. **Boxing:** He won 3 boxing titles: middleweight, light-heavyweight and heavyweight. His name was _____? (*answer p.80*)

753. **Track:** To preserve his amateur standing, he was installed as the proprietor of a Toronto cigar store (1908), even though he was a heavy smoker. (*answer p.126*)

754. **Hockey:** Traded by Toe Blake, (1963) this Vezina Trophy winner quit hockey - temporarily - after only 1 year with the NY Rangers. (*answer p.186*)

755. **Tennis:** After her Wimbledon triumph in 1957, _____ was given a Broadway ticker-tape parade in New York. (*answer p.4*)

756. **Figure Skating:** Daughter of a world champion cyclist, _____ became (1930's) the world's first female millionaire athlete. (*answer p.74*)

757. **Boxing:** He defeated Jake Kilrain by a knockout (1889) ... in the 75th round. (*answer p.172*)

758. **Track:** In 3 Olympiads, 1920-24-28, he won 9 gold and 3 silver medals in middle distance competition. He was _____? (*answer p.190*)

759. **Tennis:** In her last pro year (1980), she garnered $298,000 - lost much of it on a magazine venture and World Team Tennis. (*answer p.196*)

760. **Boxing:** :He took the world featherweight championship away from Petey Sarron in 1937 but never defended that title. (*answer p.148*)

EDDIE ARCARO

Page 153

761. **Figure Skating:** To honor her Olympic victory, the city of Ottawa presented _____ with a car bearing, the license plate 48-U-1. (*answer p.28*)

762. **Swimming:** When he was 10 (1956), he held the US 20-yard backstroke record for boys under 10. (*answer p.54*)

763. **Tennis:** By the time she turned pro in 1973 (she was 31), she'd won 61 international titles in singles, doubles and mixed doubles. (*answer p.118*)

764. **Boxing:** He made his reputation with the nickname of "The Boston Tar Baby". Who was this Weymouth, N.S. native? (*answer p.64*)

765. **Track:** First president of the NFL (founded 1920), decathlon and baseball star, _____ was named the U.S.'s Greatest Sportsman of the half-century in 1950. (*answer p.30*)

766. **Basketball:** A member of the Boston Celtics, _____ won the NBA's Most Valuable Player award 5 times. (*answer p.8*)

767. **Football:** _____ retired in 1953, came back in 1959 to coach the NY Titans for 3 years - but didn't enjoy coaching. (*answer p.182*)

768. **Boxing:** After retiring in 1979, he tried a comeback against Larry Holmes but lost on a TKO in 1980. (*answer p.162*)

769. **Soccer:** Enticed by a vastly greater pay cheque, he left River Plate and signed with Los Millionarios of Bogota in 1949, helped them win 2 league titles. (*answer p.116.*)

770. **Hockey:** His last year in goal was (1970) with the NY Rangers, though he originally "retired" (1957) in Boston. Who was this reluctant retiree? (*answer p.76*)

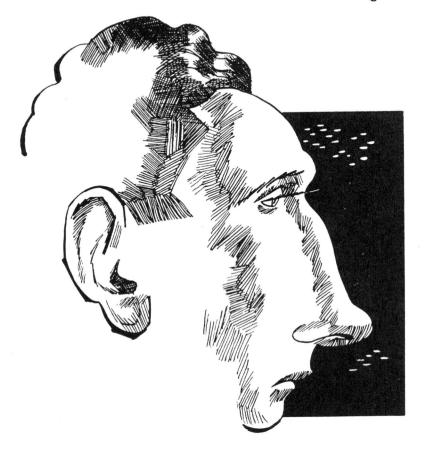

GLEN CUNNINGHAM

771. **Football:** Over 12 years, _____ led his Chicago team to 5 NFL division titles and 4 world championships. (***answer p.112***)

772. **Track:** Born 1908, this 20-year old athlete was the only Canadian to win both the 100 and 200 meter Olympic races. Name him. (***answer p.50***)

773. **Soccer:** In 1974, _____ came out of retirement to join The NY Cosmos, giving North American soccer a tremendous boost. (***answer p.66***)

774. **Boxing:** Born (1881) in Hanover, Ontario, he did not fight under his real name, which was Noah Bruno. Who was he? (***answer p.180***)

775. **Tennis:** This world champion wrote 14 (forgotten) books and several stage plays - in some of which he starred. Who was this failed author/actor? (***answer p.46***)

776. **Hockey:** Playing in the net for the Canadiens for 373 games (1910-1925) he never missed a match. (***answer p.34***)

777. **Tennis:** Between 1927 and 1935, _____ captured the Wimbledon women's singles crown 7 times. (***answer p.60***)

778. **Football:** He threw 32 TD passes to lead his team to its 2nd straight NFL title in 1959 - breaking a 16-year-old passing record. (***answer p.62***)

779. **Hockey:** He was a spark plug of the Toronto Maitlands when they won the Ontario Amateur Lacrosse League championship in 1922. (***answer p.158***)

780. **Baseball:** His toe broken by a line drive in the 1937 All Star game, this Cardinal pitcher was forced to adopt an unnatural style, permanently injuring his arm. (***answer p.132***)

GROVER
CLEVELAND ALEXANDER

781. **Tennis:** In 1933, he won the first of 3 US championships by beating Australian Jack Crawford. (**answer p.72)**

782. **Football:** He set the all-time NFL record (up to 1953) for completed passes ... 187. Who was this slinger? (**answer p.182)**

783. **Baseball:** In 1927, _____ broke his own home run record, slugging 60 round-trippers. (**answer p.44)**

784. **Boxing:** Lightweight champion Sammy Mandell defeated him in their 1st bout (1928) but Canadian_____ won a later rematch in a non-title fight.(**answer p.48**)

785. **Jockeys:** In 1967, he reached the $3 million mark - rode Damascus to the Horse of the Year title. (**answer p.58)**

786. **Swimming:** In 10 years of amateur swimming, he never lost a race in distances from 50 yards to 1/2 mile. (**answer p.86)**

787. **Baseball:** Pitching for the Pittsburgh Crawfords of the Negro National League (1924) he set a record of 30 wins against 1 loss in his 1st year. (**answer p.68)**

788. **Boxing:** He fought 5 matches against "The Bronx Bull", Jake La Motta - lost the first, won all the others. Who was this bullfighter? (**answer p.36)**

789. **Soccer:** He played inside-left on the English team which won the World Cup, beating W. Germany 4-2 in 1966. (**answer p.78)**

790. **Golf:** At the age of 20 (1922), he won the U.S. Open with a 288 score - repeated the score 36 years later. (**answer p.6)**

LIONEL CONACHER

791. **Boxing:** _____ won the heavyweight championship in 1937 by knocking out James J. Braddock in 8 rounds. (***answer p.110***)

792. **Baseball:** He broke into pro ball in 1935 with the San Diego Padres, at a salary of $150 a month. Who was this future Boston great? (***answer p.32***)

793. **Football:** But for a fracture in 1970, Saskatchewan fullback _____ would have recorded 12 straight seasons of over 1000 yards rushing. (***answer p.130***)

794. **Jockeys:** Owing the US gov't more than $1 million in income taxes, he chose to ride in Hong Kong (1977) where he did not do well. (***answer p.168***)

795. **Boxing:** This ex-heavyweight champion continued active boxing till the age of 50 (1928) even fought short exhibition bouts at 67. (***answer p.90***)

796. **Basketball:** This super center bought a Washington D.C. home for the Hanati Moslems - 7 persons were murdered there (1973), perhaps by a rival religious group. (***answer p.40***)

797. **Baseball:** This pitcher was traded to Cincinnati by Giant manager John McGraw to become a player-coach (1916). (***answer p.2***)

798. **Boxing:** Retiring (1928) as the first undefeated heavyweight champion, _____ became a lecturer on literature, a friend of George Bernard Shaw. (***answer p.24***)

799. **Soccer:** When he asked to be traded (1938), hometown Stoke City fans demonstrated so vigorously he remained for another 9 years. (***answer p.42***)

800. **Tennis:** In her first appearance at Wimbledon, aged 20, she won the women's singles title (1919). (***answer p.142***)

BUSTER CRABBE

801. **Baseball:** In 1979, _____ surpassed Frank Frisch's major league record of 2880 hits by a switch-hitter. (**answer p.22**)

802. **Boxing:** His manager, "Doc" Kearns, secretly sprinkled plaster of paris on his wet bandaged hand before his heavyweight title fight in Toledo, Ohio, 1919. Whose hands were they? (**answer p.108**)

803. **Boxing:** He was the first world heavyweight champion to fight under Marquis of Queensbury rules (1892). Who was this gloved titleholder? (**answer p.172**)

804. **Hockey:** During his 10 years with the Montreal Canadiens (1952-62), they won 5 straight Stanley Cups while _____ won the Vezina Trophy 5 times. (**answer p.186**)

805. **Baseball:** Jack Dunn, owner of the Baltimore Orioles, adopted him in 1914, then sold him to the Boston Red Sox as a pitcher. (**answer p.44**)

806. **Tennis:** In 1936 she won the first of 4 consecutive US national amateur championships. (**answer p.38**)

807. **Football:** He appeared in 2 Hollywood movies: "King of the Texas Rangers" and "Triple Threat". Who was this unremarkable actor? (**answer p.182**)

808. **Swimming:** Enrolled at 17 in the dentistry course at Indiana U., he gave it all up to train for the 1968 Olympics. Who was dentistry's loss, swimming's gain? (**answer p.192**)

809. **Tennis:** At the age of 17, she defeated Maria Bueno (1960) to win the Australian crown, the first of 10 consecutive triumphs. (**answer p.118**)

810. **Jockeys:** In 1955, aged 23, he won the US national jockey title. (**answer p.168**)

MUHAMMAD ALI

811. **Baseball:** He was given the names "Jay Hanna" at birth (1921), but became known as "Jerome Herman", by his own choice. He was usually called _____. (*answer p.132*)

812. **Football:** Winner of the Hickock Award as the outstanding pro athlete of 1964 _____ set a career record of 756 points, the highest ever for a non-kicker. (*answer p.96*)

813. **Baseball:** In the late 30's, this Dodger star-to-be was a UCLA whiz in track, football, basketball - and baseball. Who was this whiz? (*answer p.56*)

814. **Boxing:** In his entire pro career (1915-1928), he lost only 1 bout in 77 - to Harry Greb. Who was this one-time loser? (*answer p.24*)

815. **Swimming:** A documentary film about his career was made titled "The Boy Who Swims Like A Fish." Who was the boy? (*answer p.54*)

816. **Track:** The US Amateur Athletic Union declared him a professional (1907) because he was supported by the Irish-Canadian Athletic Club. (*answer p.126*)

817. **Football:** The day he retired (1978), _____ was appointed head coach of the team he was leaving, the Saskatchewan Roughriders. (*answer p.88*)

818. **Soccer:** Barcelona bought his services from Amsterdam Ajax in 1973 for over a million dollars - and paid him a similar amount. (*answer p.10*)

819. **Golf:** Because of his life style he became known as "Sir Walter." What was his name? (*answer p.20*)

820. **Tennis:** Born in 1921, he won his first title at the age of 15 in the Culver Military Academy tournament. (*answer p.16*)

BOB COUSY

821. **Soccer:** He became manager of the Greek champions Panathinaikos, took them to the European Cup final in 1971 (*answer p.106*)

822. **Track:** This middle distance marvel invaded the USA in 1925, set 34 indoor records in 16 days. Who was this Finnish firster? (*answer p.190*)

823. **Basketball:** He held the NBA's all-time scoring record of 13,419 points until the 1983-84 season. Who was the high scorer? (*answer p.188*)

824. **Baseball:** With Cobb, Ruth, Johnson and Mathewson this shortstop was elected to the Hall of Fame when it was established in 1936. He was _____? (*answer p.122*)

825. **Football:** Perhaps the game most remembered by many fans was the one in which this quarterback's team was beaten 73-0 by the Chicago Bears (1940). (*answer p.182*)

826. **Soccer:** This Manchester player claimed to have bedded over 1,000 girls, was sued for breach of promise. Who was this defendant? (*answer p.200*)

827. **Jockeys:** This English jockey won 21 French classics including the famous Arc de Triomphe 3 times. He was _____? (*answer p.98*)

828. **Hockey:** Born in Toronto, _____ played defense on 2 Stanley Cup winners: Chicago in 1934 and Montreal Maroons in 1935. (*answer p.158*)

829. **Swimming:** The world's best competitive swimmer, _____ also played on medal-winning water polo teams in the 1924 and 1928 Olympics. (*answer p.86*)

830. **Baseball:** In 1 game in 1932 this Yankee hit 4 consecutive home runs. (*answer p.184*)

RUSS JACKSON

831. **Tennis:** He scored the first "Grand Slam" of tennis in 1938, sweeping the Australian, French, British and US championships. What was this slammer's name? (*answer p.92*)

832. **Baseball:** This right-hander is still considered as having the fastest ball of all-time _____ at over 120 m.p.h. Who was the speed king? (*answer p.102.*)

833. **Boxing:** Rarely weighing over 170 lbs. this future heavyweight champion was early apprenticed to a blacksmith, developing his powerful shoulders and back. (*answer p.80*)

834. **Baseball:** Clark Griffith considered signing him for the Washington Senators (in the 30's) but backed away from trying to break the major league's color bar. (*answer p.198*)

835. **Golf:** Son of a Texas junk dealer, he became a caddy at 11, a full pro at 19, but didn't win a tournament for 7 years. (*answer p.84*)

836. **Baseball:** Returning from military service in 1945, Cleveland's _____ resumed his winning ways - at the record pitcher's salary of $80,000 a year. (*answer p.94*)

837. **Soccer:** In 1966, AC Milan offered Bayern, Munich over 1/2 a million dollars for this centre-half who was _____? (*answer p.134*)

838. **Football:** "On the field _____ is the equal of 3 football players and a horse", said Damon Runyon. (*answer p.140*)

839. **Hockey:** This center's nickname was "Le Gros Bill". What was his real name? (*answer p.174*)

840. **Football:** This Saskatchewan CFL fullback won the Schenley (Most Valuable Player) Award in 1965, was runner-up in 1968 and 1969. (*answer p.130*)

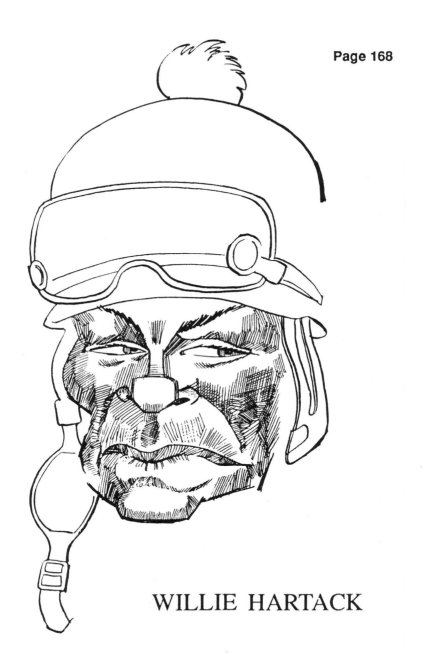

WILLIE HARTACK

841. **Boxing:** Born in 1895 _____ became a famous Broadway restauranteur .... as well as a feared heavyweight champion. (*answer p.108*)

842. **Baseball:** In 1899, he was drafted by Cincinnati and then traded to John McGraw's NY Giants for veteran pitcher Amos Rusie. (*answer p.2*)

843. **Golf:** Born in Ashford, Virginia in 1912, he won the Masters 3 times the PGA 3 times and was the game's top money-winner 3 times. (*answer p.124*)

844. **Tennis:** Although humiliated by Lew Hoad and Ken Rosewall in his first 2 years as a pro, by 1965 he established himself as no. 1. (*answer p.146*)

845. **Baseball:** Over 23 consecutive years _____ hit 10 or more home runs for the Milwaukee/Atlanta Braves. (*answer p.82*)

846. **Figure Skating:** She won a gold medal in the 1968 Grenoble Winter Olympics - the only US athlete to do so. What was the name of this golden girl? (*answer p.128*)

847. **Jockeys:** In 1975, he was awarded the Order of the British Empire - after winning over 3,000 races, some for The Queen herself. Who was this royal favourite? (*answer p.98*)

848. **Baseball:** He became the playing manager of the Detroit Tigers in 1921 and remained in the job for 6 years. Who was he? (*answer p.12*)

849. **Jockeys:** His prickly manner earned him the sobriquet of "Little Hard Tack". What was his name? (*answer p.168*)

850. **Boxing:** He was the first lightweight champion to earn a million dollars in the ring - and the only one to retire undefeated (1925). (*answer p.194*)

WILLIE MAYS

851. **Baseball:** In 1974 he broke the prevailing big league home run record of 714 - to the accompaniment of hate mail from white racist fans. Whose name was on the envelopes? (***answer p.82)***

852. **Golf:** Golf's greatest showman, he travelled with servants and a huge luxury car in which he was frequently served a champagne lunch. (***answer p.20)***

853. **Tennis:** _____ was the first Englishman to win the Wimbledon Singles (1933) since A. W. Gore in 1909. (***answer p.72)***

854. **Football:** His team defeated that of another famous passer in 1940 by a score of 73-0 to win the NFL title. He was Chicago Bear _____? (***answer p.112*)**

855. **Swimming:** This superstar's mother was Martha Dent Perry - she doubled for Maureen O'Sullivan swim sequences in Tarzan films. Who was her son? (***answer p.54)***

856. **Boxing:** To avoid US anti-boxing laws, he fought a bout at a secret Mexican location in 1896, defending his middleweight title against Peter Maher in a 95-second KO. (***answer p.80)***

857. **Soccer:** When he was only 15 (1953), 18 different English clubs wanted to sign him - Matt Busby got him for Manchester United. (***answer p.78)***

858. **Baseball:** Playing for the Birmingham, Ala. Black Barons, aged 17, _____ was spotted and signed by a NY Giant scout (1948). (***answer p.170)***

859. **Baseball:** NL president Ford Frick called the bluff of the Phillies and Cardinals when they threatened to strike if this black player, _____ , remained in the league (1947). (***answer p.56)***

860. **Hockey:** He was traded from Winnipeg to Hartford in 1980, but retired when his lady friend was seriously hurt in an auto accident. (***answer p.178)***

JOHN L.
SULLIVAN

861. **Golf:** "Follow the Sun" was the name of a film starring Glen Ford. Whose life story did it present? (***answer p.84)***

862. **Hockey:** His greatest goal came in an NHL semi-final game against Boston in 1952 when he scored Montreal's winner after being knocked out for several minutes. (***answer p.14)***

863. **Boxing:** Born (1912) in Columbus, Mississippi, he fought his first amateur bouts under the name "Melody Jackson". What was his non-musical name? (***answer p.148)***

864. **Track:** Within 3/4 of an hour, he set 4 world records in a Big Ten track meet on May 25, 1935. He was _____? (***answer p.104)***

865. **Tennis:** She was largely responsible for the establishment of the women - only pro tour in the 70's. Who was this court monarch? (***answer p.196)***

866. **Football:** _____ quarterbacked the NY Jets to the Super Bowl championship (1969) over the Baltimore Colts. (***answer p.150)***

867. **Basketball:** In 1973 he left the NBA to join the San Diego Conquistadors as player-coach for $600,000. (***answer p.188)***

868. **Tennis:** Born in Germantown, Pa. (1893), he was the first pro to earn $1 million - despite the loss of a finger on his playing hand. (***answer p.46)***

869. **Baseball:** He was the first AL player to reach an annual salary of $100,000 (1949). Who was this NY Yankee? (***answer p. 144***)

870. **Swimming:** He and an equally famous swimmer/movie star Johnny Weismuller portrayed a film water fight in "Swampfire" - both turned blue in the 54° F water. (***answer p.160)***

JEAN BELIVEAU

871. Basketball: He started his career on an athletic scholarship at San Francisco U. (1954). Whose team was known as the "Homeless Dons"? (***answer p.8***)

872. Football: After 2 unsuccessful years as coach of the Saskatchewan Roughriders, he was let go - to become a full-time sportscaster in Regina. (***answer p.88***)

873. Basketball: He left the NBA in 1963 to coach the lowly Boston College Eagles - they won 117 games, lost 34 in his 6 years with them. (***answer p.164***)

874. Baseball: He played for the NY Yankees as an outfielder in 10 World Series in the 30's and 40's. (***answer p.144***)

875. Tennis: Urged on by his brother he entered the California State Championship in 1930, won it at the age of 15. (***answer p.92***)

876. Football: Born (1936) in St. Simons, Georgia, he established a NFL record 106 touchdowns by rushing (starting in 1957). (***answer p.96***)

877. Boxing: This Detroit heavyweight became known as "The Brown Bomber". Who was this high-flyer? (***answer p.110***)

878. Golf: His 230–yd double eagle shot in the 1935 Masters Tournament may well be the most famous single shot in golf history. (***answer p.6***)

879. Basketball: Despite this Los Angeles Laker's scoring records his team did not win an NBA championship till 1972. (***answer p.188***)

880. Football: Due to a leg injury, Baltimore's 41-year-old _____ was forced to call it a day in 1974. (***answer p. 62***)

BOBBY
JONES

881. **Soccer:** Born in Buenos Aires he became a professional on Argentina's River Plate team in 1945 at the age of 19. He was _____? (*answer p.116*)

882. **Football:** In 1978, a panel of 16 veteran reporters from 9 cities named _____ the CFL's most outstanding player of the previous quarter-century. (*answer p.70*)

883. **Tennis:** The Los Angeles Tennis Club lured him away from Culver Military Academy - he was then National Boys Champion - by offering him lessons from Ellsworth Vines. (*answer p.16*)

884. **Boxing:** Famous for his free spending and high living, heavyweight champion _____ lost his title in 1892, later became a teetotalling preacher. (*answer p.172*)

885. **Jockeys:** Starting in 1941, he had mounts on 10 Horses of the Year - no other jockey had had more than 2. (*answer p.152*)

886. **Golf:** This Georgia amateur won 120 golf cups, including his first, captured at the age of 6 (1908). (*answer p.176*)

887. **Hockey:** "I'm glad I won it now (the Norris Trophy for best defenseman 1966-67)," said Harry Howell, "from now on it's going to belong to _____". (*answer p.100*)

888. **Football:** In 1926 this halfback and C. C. Pyle founded the American Football League. He was? (*answer p.140*)

889. **Jockeys:** He won his first Kentucky Derby on a horse called Lawrin on May 7, 1938. Who was the rider? (*answer p.152*)

890. **Soccer:** In 1972 he was named European Footballer of The Year. Who was this West German star? (*answer p.134*)

BOBBY HULL

891. **Golf:** Sponsored by the A. G. Spalding Co. he helped popularize golf by touring in the US (1900) losing only 1 of dozens of exhibition matches. (**answer p.26**)

892. **Boxing:** This ex-champion's comeback was stopped (after 18 wins and 1 draw in 2 years) by Jimmy McLarnin in a 6th round KO (1932). (**answer p.194**)

893. **Football:** The NY Jets paid _____ $427,000 to join them in 1965 - the highest ever pro football salary. (**answer p.150**)

894. **Swimming:** In 2 Olympiads, 1924 and 1928, he won a total of 5 Olympic golds and 1 bronze. Who was this Tarzan of the pool? (**answer p.86**)

895. **Baseball:** On his retirement as a player in 1976, he became director of player personnel and vice-president of The Atlanta Braves. (**answer p.82**)

896. **Tennis:** She grew up in New York slums but went on to win both the Wimbledon and US championships in 1957 and 1958. (**answer p.4**)

897. **Soccer:** The Brazilian government declared _____ "a national monument", not to be traded, despite European offers to him of up to $2 million. (**answer p.66**)

898. **Figure Skating:** Her Olympic gold in 1948 was the first ever for a North American skater. Her name was _____? (**answer p.28**)

899. **Baseball:** Over 14 years this Yankee hit 493 home runs, going over 40 5 times. He was 1st baseman _____. (**answer p.184**)

900. **Basketball:** He retired as a player in 1968, after his team defeated the Los Angeles Lakers for the NBA title. (**answer p.8**)

TOMMY BURNS

901. **Soccer:** His hometown of Tres Corãcoes (Three Hearts) erected a great statue in his honor in 1971. Of whom is this statue? (***answer p.66***)

902. **Jockeys:** This English-born jockey surpassed Sir Gordon Richard's total of 4,870 wins by 1,162. (***answer p.18***)

903. **Swimming:** He was the star of the 1972 Munich Olympic Games in which 9 Israeli athletes were murdered. (***answer p.192***)

904. **Boxing:** As an amateur in the late 30's, this Harlem youngster compiled a record of 90 wins in a row, 70 by K.O.'s. (***answer p.36***)

905. **Track:** In the 1936 Olympic games, he won an unprecedented 4 gold medals. Who was this US medalist? (***answer p.104***)

906. **Baseball:** This Chicago Cub hurler was drafted into the US army in 1918, served in France in World War I. (***answer p.156***)

907. **Football:** He appeared in movies with stars such as Richard Burton, Paul Newman, Sophia Loren and James Brolin. (***answer p.120***)

908. **Boxing:** He lost his American light heavyweight title to Windmill Harry Greg in 1922, regained it 9 months later. (***answer p.24***)

909. **Baseball:** After winning 28 games in 1935, he signed with the Cardinals for $25,005 - making him the big leagues' highest paid pitcher by $5. (***answer p.132***)

910. **Figure Skating:** A star of several touring ice shows she did sugarless gum, pantyhose commercials - became a sports commentator for NBC and ABC. (***answer p.128***)

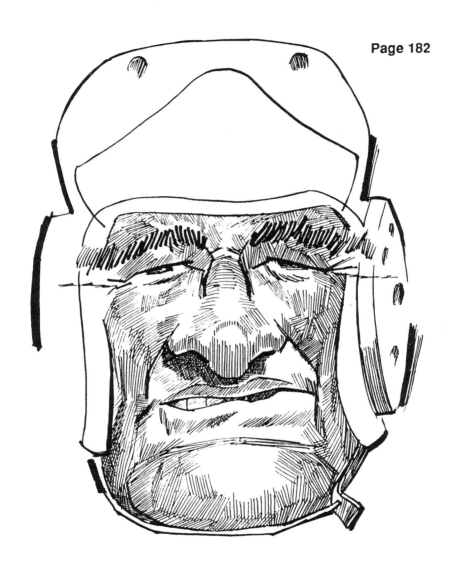

SAMMY BAUGH

911. Tennis: Over 7 years (1919-26)_____won 6 All-England titles, 6 French championships, 6 Wimbledon doubles, 2 French doubles, 3 Wimbledon and 2 French mixed doubles. (***answer p.142)***

912. Golf: He and Bobby Jones both qualified at the age of 19 for the U. S. Open - neither did well (1921). (***answer p.6)***

913. Jockeys: After winning the English Derby at 18 (1948), he was suspended for 6 months for endangering Sir Gordon Richards at Ascot. (***answer p.98)***

914. Baseball: In 1929 he played with the Crawford Colored Giants, a semi-pro team which passed the hat amongst spectators to pay their players a few dollars per game. (***answer p.198)***

915. Baseball: Born in San Diego, Ca. (1918), his athletic nickname was "The Splendid Splinter." Otherwise he was called _____. (***answer p.32)***

916. Track: After a disappointing showing in the Los Angeles 1932 Olympics, this Vancouver sprinter became an RCAF pilot instructor, then went into the insurance business. (***answer p.50***)

917. Football: This NFL fullback gained a career record 12,312 yards rushing averaging 5.2 yards per carry. (***answer p.96)***

918. Soccer: This Ajax player became the first guilder millionaire in Holland in 1971, guaranteeing him 1.5 million guilders over 7 years. (***answer p.10)***

919. Baseball: Detroit outfielder_____won 9 consecutive AL batting championships, then finished 2nd, then proceeded to win 3 more in a row. (***answer p.12)***

920. Golf: A year after being told he might never walk again _____ won the US Open (1950) for a 2nd time. (***answer p.84)***

LOU
GEHRIG

921. **Tennis:** At the age of 21, he achieved international notice by winning the Argentine championship in 1930. Who was this English amateur? (*answer p.72)*

922. **Boxing:** This ex-champion's comeback came to an end at the hands of Rocky Marciano in 1951. Who was this 8th round KO victim? (*answer p.110)*

923. **Swimming:** As a result of his victories in the 1964 Olympics, _____ was named US and World Athlete of the Year. (*answer p.54)*

924. **Basketball:** As a rebounder, he led the NBA 4 times, finished 2nd 5 times between 1956 and 1966. Who was this rebounder? (*answer p.8)*

925. **Tennis:** A TV commentator, coach of the US Davis Cup team, he was the 3rd former player to be elected to the Hall of Fame - after Arthur Ashe and Don Budge (1985). (*answer p.16*)

926. **Golf:** Only 8 years elapsed from the time _____ won his first title to his last (1923-30). (*answer p.176)*

927. **Boxing:** This heavyweight champion was dethroned by a KO (1892) at the hands of Gentleman Jim Corbett. He was _____? (*answer p.172)*

928. **Tennis:** After leaving competitive tennis (1938), she turned to writing, painting, interior and fashion design. (*answer p.60)*

929. **Baseball:** This NL pitching great became a member of the US Army of Occupation, was accidentally exposed to poison gas (1919), later developed tuberculosis. (*answer p.2*)

930. **Soccer:** In 1963 he was signed by Matt Busby of Manchester United. Who was this 17 year-old? (*answer p.200)*

JACQUES PLANTE

931. **Tennis:** After winning the US singles title in 1938, she made her debut as a supper club singer in New York's Waldorf Astoria Hotel. Who was this songstress? (*answer p.38*)

932. **Figure Skating:** After her Olympic victory in 1948, she turned pro, set up a foundation to aid crippled children with her earnings. (*answer p.28*)

933. **Hockey:** Born in 1928 in Floral, Saskatchewan, he was the first NHL player to reach a total of 600 goals (1965). What was his name? (*answer p.136*)

934. **Baseball:** In 1946 he set a major league strikeout record by fanning 348 batters in one season. Who was this fan-tastic pitcher? (*answer p.94*)

935. **Basketball:** _____ won the NBA Rookie of the Year award after turning pro with the Cincinnati Royals in 1960. (*answer p.138*)

936. **Track:** He won 3 consecutive 15-mile Toronto "marathons" (1906-7-8). His name had an aquatic flavour. What was it? (*answer p.126*)

937. **Baseball:** Chosen Sporting News' Player of the Decade (60's), _____ was named to the NL all-star team every year from 1954 to 1973. (*answer p.170*)

938. **Soccer:** His team whipped England 6-3 in 1953, the first time the latter had been beaten at home in international competition. (*answer p.106*)

939. **Boxing:** In 1922, this lightweight champion lost his bid for the welterweight title of champion Jack Britton. He was _____? (*answer p.194*)

940. **Golf:** He was the PGA tour's leading money winner in 1938, 1949 and 1950. (*answer p.124*)

WILT CHAMBERLAIN

941. **Tennis:** Deeply involved in the Women's Liberation Movement this star was nicknamed "Mother Freedom". What was her non-maternal name? (*answer p.196*)

942. **Jockeys:** His favourite ride was Count Fleet, which _____ rode to the Triple Crown in 1943. Who was this rider? (*answer p.18*)

943. **Baseball:** In 1941 _____ set a major league record by hitting in 56 consecutive games, missed one, then ran up another string of 17. (*answer p.144*)

944. **Boxing:** Born in 1896 in New York, his true name was Benjamin Leiner. What was the ring name by which he became famous? (*answer p.194*)

945. **Baseball:** This Yankee established an all-time record of 23 grand slam home runs. (*answer p.184*)

946. **Hockey:** He won the NHL's Vezina Trophy from 1956 through 1960 and again in 1962 and 1969. (*answer p.186*)

947. **Tennis:** _____'s first "Grand Slam" came in 1962. He defeated countryman Roy Emerson 4 times in the process. (*answer p.146*)

948. **Baseball:** Playing for Cincinnati, he led NL outfielders' averages 3 times, 3rd basemen once. (*answer p.22*)

949. **Skating:** No athlete ever earned as much as she did - 50 million dollars plus for films and various other commercial ventures. (*answer p.74*)

950. **Track:** In 1930, he set a new US interscholastic mile record of 4:24.7, running for Kansas University. Who was this collegian? (*answer p.154*)

PAAVO NURMI

951. **Hockey:** In 1962, this Chicago left-winger scored 50 goals, to equal the previous record of only 2 other NHL players. (*answer p.178)*

952. **Boxing:** In his first official fight he won the Canadian light-heavyweight championship in 1920. (*answer p.158)*

953. **Baseball:** In 1957, while still pitching, he appeared in a movie with Robert Mitchum, titled "The Wonderful Country". Who was this throwing thespian? (*answer p.68)*

954. **Hockey:** Traded by Detroit to Toronto for $20,000 (1964), _____ and Johnny Bower sparked the Leafs to the Stanley Cup in 1967. (*answer p.76)*

955. **Football:** "You and Jesus Christ are the only 2 people I'd ever pay that much money ($10,000) to." To whom did George Halas say this? (*answer p.112)*

956. **Soccer:** Over his 18-year (1955-73) career, _____ garnered a record 105 "caps" playing for England. (*answer p.78)*

957. **Track:** Born in 1888, his Indian name was "Bright Path". What did the rest of the world call him? (*answer p.30)*

958. **Boxing:** Born in 1880, he ran away from his Nova Scotia home after a paternal beating, made his way to Boston - he was 12. (*answer p.64)*

959. **Football:** In 1964, the Chicago Cubs offered this college quarterback $50,000 to play baseball for them. (*answer p.150*)

960. **Figure Skating:** Born 1913 in Oslo, she won the women's figure skating championship of the world in 1927. (*answer p.74)*

MARK
SPITZ

961. Boxing: After losing to Gene Tunney, he made the famous remark "I forgot to duck," in explanation. (*answer p.108*)

962. Basketball: As a gesture against sport's racist attitudes, he boycotted the US Olympic team in '68. Who was this protester? (*answer p.40*)

963. Football: As a Saskatchewan Roughrider rusher, he carried for a record 16, 116 yards. (*answer p.130*)

964. Baseball: 4,191 was his lifetime total of base hits of which 118 were home runs. (*answer p.12*)

965. Hockey: When he quit the Canadiens in 1960, _____ held or shared 33 NHL scoring records. (*answer p.14*)

966. Tennis: Born in 1938 in Australia he dropped out of school at 15, determined to pursue a career in tennis. (*answer p.146*)

967. Boxing: This heavyweight champion successfully defended his title 12 times in 2 years, 1906 - 1908. (*answer p.180*)

968. Baseball: He was the major·league pitcher who invented the "screwball" in the early 1900's. What was the inventor's name? (*answer p.2*)

969. Track: Winning 2 races in 1935, he set 4 world records: the 220-yard and 200-meters - and the 220-yard hurdles and the 200-meter hurdles. (*answer p.104*)

970. Tennis: The world's foremost player at the time, _____ joined the US Air Force in 1941, remained in it for 5 years. (*answer p.92*)

BENNY LEONARD

971. Boxing: He was the first of many black fighters to win the world heavyweight championship. Who was he? (***answer p.90)***

972. Hockey: Playing alongside his equally famous Montreal Canadien colleague, he won the NHL scoring title in 1956. (***answer p.174)***

973. Boxing: _____ retired as undefeated heavyweight champion of the world in 1949. (***answer p.110)***

974. Jockeys: Born in Fabens, Texas (1931) _____ was an early arrival even as a baby, 1 month premature and weighing only 2 1/2 lbs. (***answer p.58***)

975. Baseball: A non-smoker, he forced the withdrawal of a cigarette baseball card of himself - a card now valued at over $1500. Whose portrait does it carry? (***answer p.122)***

976. Tennis: In 3 separate years, 1963, 1965 and 1969 she won 3 of the 4 major open titles but the Slam eluded her till later. (***answer p.118)***

977. Boxing: Born (1920) in Detroit, Michigan, his name was Walker Smith. What was his ring name? (***answer p.36)***

978. Soccer: Though his driving licence was suspended for traffic violations, his income while playing for Manchester rose to over $200,000 a year. (***answer p.200)***

979. Golf: _____ made professional golf what it is ... he broke down the walls of prejudice (against the professional golfer). (***answer p.20)***

980. Basketball: Against the NY Knicks he scored 100 points in one game in 1962. Who was this Philadelphia Warrior? (***answer p.188)***

BILLIE JEAN KING

981. **Baseball:** A football star (1922), Columbia grad _____ was also a brilliant pitcher but later made his name as a Yankee first baseman. (***answer p.184***)

982. **Football:** Playing fullback for the Cleveland Browns, he became (1963) the first player to rush for more than a mile in 1 season. What was this miler's name? (***answer p.96)***

983. **Baseball:** This future St Louis Cardinal's education in Chickalah, Arkansas extended only as far as the first 2 grades. Who was this uneducated flinger? (***answer p.132)***

984. **Soccer:** He retired (1974) in Europe, was coaxed out of retirement 5 years later to join the LA Aztecs. Who was this retiring forward? (***answer p.10)***

985. **Tennis:** After a short pro tennis career, she turned to pro golf, earned a fair living till the mid-1970's. (***answer p.4)***

986. **Baseball:** He won more games than any other American League pitcher - 416. Who was he? (***answer p.102)***

987. **Boxing:** _____ won (1881) the world heavyweight championship at the age of 23, knocking out Paddy Ryan in the ninth round. (***answer p.172)***

988. **Jockeys:** _____ was the first jockey to earn more than $2 million in a year, winning $2,343,955 in 1956. (***answer p.168)***

989. **Baseball:** This Yankee star appeared in 2 films: "Goin'Home" and "Pride of the Yankees". Who was this part-time actor? (***answer p.44)***

990. **Soccer:** Real Madrid coaxed him away from Bogota, Columbia in 1953, later made the world's highest-paid player. (***answer p.116)***

JOSH GIBSON

991. **Baseball:** At 19, he established a major league strikeout record (1937) by fanning 18 Detroit Tiger batters. Who was this Tiger-Tamer? (*answer p.94)*

992. **Football:** A native of Hamilton (Ontario), _____ was offered a Rhodes Scholarship - turned it down to play pro football. What was this scholar's name? (*answer p.166)*

993. **Track:** At 15, (1923) he was stricken with rheumatic fever and doctors told this Vancouver sprinter to forget about a track career. _____ didn't. (*answer p.50)*

994. **Boxing:** After winning the world welterweight crown (1938), he conquered Lou Ambers to win the lightweight title in the same year. (*answer p.148)*

995. **Jockeys:** After retirement in 1961, he became a representative for a company making electronic betting equipment. (*answer p.152)*

996. **Golf:** Possessor of an engineering degree, he never became an engineer but later graduated in law, became a successful Georgia attorney. (*answer p.176)*

997. **Boxing:** When he retired in 1925, he had held his title longer than any other lightweight champion - 7 years, 7 months, 18 days. (*answer p.194)*

998. **Tennis:** In the 40's he won most amateur major international titles but was forced to take a job in a meat-packing firm for $60 a week. (*answer p.16)*

999. **Basketball:** In 1962, _____ was voted the NBA's all-time number one player in a poll of 100 sports editors. (*answer p.164)*

1000. **Boxing:** He lost his heavyweight title to James J. Jeffries in 1899. Jeffries was 13 years younger, 40 lbs heavier than _____? (*answer p.80)*

GEORGE BEST